IT'S IN THE DETAILS

SMALL THINGS THAT CHANGE EVERYTHING

Dr. Danita Johnson Woods

It's in the Details: Small Things That Change Everything
by Dr. Danita Johnson Woods

Published by Woods World Publishers, Inc.
Cover and book design by Nick Zelinger, NZGraphics.com

ISBN:
978-0-9972124-7-1 (Hard cover)
978-0-9972124-8-8 (Paperback)
978-0-9972124-9-5 (E-book)

Library of Congress Control Number: 2026905755

Published by Woods World Publishing

First Edition

Printed in the United States of America

Author's Note

This book was born from a deep belief: that the smallest things often carry the greatest weight. A gesture. A glance. A comma. A missed appointment. An overlooked deadline. A policy line. A forgotten name. Each chapter is a reflection on the quiet forces that shape our lives—sometimes invisibly, often powerfully.

Many personal stories shared in this book come from people I deeply love and admire. Their experiences and reflections beautifully embody the theme of this book: It's in the Details. Each story invites us to pause, notice, and appreciate the subtle moments that shape our lives.

I want to extend heartfelt thanks to those who allowed their voices, insights, and stories to become part of this journey:

Mrs. Kaufman, my first-grade teacher, who saw value in me long before I saw it in myself.

Dr. Tanya Rogers, whose courage in sharing her truth reminds us that vulnerability is strength.

Dr. Robert Rohm, mentor and friend, who introduced me to the transformative power of DISC.

Two remarkable young Gen Xers, Davion Davis and my amazing grandson, Javier Cardona, who give us reason to be proud.

Mark Spencer, an artistic genius whose stories reveal how performance and presence intertwine.

Dr. Chiedu Nchekwube, whose wisdom in integrative medicine inspires a deeper approach to healing.

Tara Robertson, my remarkable assistant, who holds things together behind the scenes with grace and precision.

Kyla Parker, my daughter, whose journey as a mother and woman is both moving and instructive.

And Michael Woods, my amazing husband, whose love, partnership, and quiet support will continue to anchor me every day.

The narratives, reflections, and branded elements throughout these pages are original. Where language echoes widely known ideas or shared cultural expressions, appropriate attribution has been provided. In places where phrasing may resemble public discourse or familiar sentiments, it is used with care, intention, and in the spirit of transformation—not replication.

This book does not aim to sensationalize, but to remember—and to remind. To offer truth-telling as an act of service, healing, and accountability. May these stories encourage you to recognize the power of details—in history, in systems, and in your own life.

INTRODUCTION
The Awakening

One crisp morning, as the first rays of sunlight filtered through my bedroom window, I found myself pondering a simple yet profound truth: it is the small details of life that shape who we are. In that quiet moment of reflection, a realization washed over me—a revelation that would serve as the cornerstone of my journey into writing this book, "It's in the Details: How Small Things Change Everything."

Before we begin, I offer this personal reflection—one that grounds the journey ahead in intention, resilience, and the power of choosing with care.

Choices

I am the sum of the choices I make.
I choose to control my own fate.
And not be deterred by opposition and hate.
I choose to learn from my mistakes.
From adversity, I choose flexibility, and so
I learn grace and humility.
I am resilient. I bounce back.
My strength allows me to stay on track.
I apply my skills and talents with exuberance,
Because I choose to strive for excellence.
I choose to embrace life.
With a palette knife, I paint my dreams.

Although to some they may seem extreme,
My dreams cannot be suppressed,
Because I choose to define my own success.
I choose to imagine the difference I can make.
The world is my oyster. I choose to partake.
And so, I celebrate the choices I make.

—Dr. Danita Johnson Woods

From childhood to adulthood, our lives are a mosaic of decisions, each influenced by nuances we often overlook. As children, we are taught to make choices, but it is the subtle details that guide our evaluations and shape our thoughts. A kind word from a teacher, a smile from a stranger, or the warmth of a home-cooked meal—these seemingly minor moments leave indelible marks on our hearts and minds.

I recalled my own experiences; moments where small details shifted my perspective. The time I hesitated at a crossroads, unsure of which path to take, only to find clarity in a second of stillness, or the sounds of nature such as a gentle rustle of leaves, or the laughter of friends nearby. These details, often dismissed as trivial, became the compass that guided my decisions, leading me to discover my passions and values.

In my quest to explore this theme, I realized that mindfulness plays a crucial role. As a young person, I often found myself yearning for instant gratification, wanting everything to happen immediately. Whether it was achieving a goal, receiving validation, or simply getting what I desired, the impatience for quick results was a constant companion. However, over time, I learned that the power of learning to wait and taking the time to think about the ramifications of choices is critical. In my efforts to guide my children and my grandchildren, I strive to instill in them the value of patience, encouraging them to appreciate the journey rather than just the destination.

When we pause to appreciate the intricacies of life, we cultivate a deeper awareness of our surroundings and ourselves. It invites us to slow down, to consider the ripple effects of our choices, and to embrace the power of intention. Each decision, no matter how small, contributes to the narrative of our lives—a narrative that deserves to be told with care and consideration.

As I delved further into the concept of detail, I recognized its impact on relationships. The small gestures—a handwritten note, a listening ear, or a shared laugh—forge connections that stand the test of time. These details enrich our interactions, reminding us that it is often the little things that create the strongest bonds.

Moreover, I discovered that creativity thrives in the realm of details. Many great innovations stem from a keen observation of the world around us. By honing our attention to the minutiae, we unlock the potential for creative breakthroughs, inspiring us to think outside the box and approach challenges with fresh perspectives. This realization has been a guiding force in my writing journey, leading me to pen not only this book but several others before it. Each project has allowed me to explore different facets of life, but the common thread has always been the importance of recognizing the small details that shape our experiences.

Culturally, the details that define our societies reflect our collective identity. They shape our beliefs, traditions, and values, influencing how we perceive the world and interact with one another. A pivotal lesson I learned from a mentor, who introduced me to Stephen Covey's wisdom, is the principle of "seek first to understand, then to be understood." This concept emphasizes the importance of listening and empathizing with others before expressing our own views. By embracing this mindset, we can foster deeper connections and cultivate a more harmonious society. Examining these details allows us to better understand ourselves and the communities we inhabit, creating a richer tapestry of human experience.

As I pen down these thoughts, I am reminded that the journey of self-discovery is often paved with small moments of clarity and insight. "It's in the Details" is not just a reflection of my experiences; it is an invitation for readers to embark on their own explorations. Together, we will uncover how the smallest details can lead to the most significant transformations, shaping our lives in ways we may never fully comprehend.

Contents

Small Moments Write the Story of Our Lives

The Quiet Power of What's Often Overlooked

"Sometimes, it isn't the grand gestures that change a life.
It's the quiet noticing, the small kindness,
the detail that reminds someone they matter."
— Dr. Danita Johnson Woods

I was just a little girl with holes in her shoes, trying not to be noticed for all the wrong reasons. But then someone did notice—not with pity, but with presence. Mrs. Kaufman saw more than a struggling student; she saw a spark worth nurturing. And one afternoon, she opened a drawer and pulled out a pair of red canvas shoes that changed everything.

They didn't fix our poverty. They didn't silence the teasing. But they gave me something rare: the quiet dignity of being seen.

This chapter isn't just about shoes or kindness. It's about how unnoticed moments can shape entire futures. Because before the boardrooms and accolades, there was a dime, a helping hand, and a gesture of grace.

Welcome to a journey where red shoes are never just red shoes—where the quietest details hold the power to transform everything.

CHAPTER ONE

The Quiet Power of What's Often Overlooked

"Transformation often begins quietly, in the small moments and subtle decisions that shape the course of our lives."
— Dr. Danita Johnson Woods

We often think of transformation as something sparked by grand gestures or sweeping changes. But the truth is, the most profound shifts—in nature, in business, in relationships, and within ourselves—begin quietly. They are born in the small moments, the subtle decisions, the unnoticed patterns that shape our lives. Like threads in a tapestry, these details may seem insignificant when viewed alone, yet together, they form the fabric of everything we experience.

The Web of Influence: How Small Becomes Significant

When I was six years old, my family moved into a small basement apartment on Polk Street in Gary, Indiana. It felt like an adventure, like opening a new book filled with blank pages just waiting for us to fill them with stories. I was excited to leave behind the old place that felt heavy and dark, hoping this new home would be brighter and happier.

As we settled in, I imagined all the fun we could have—new friends to meet, games to play, and laughter echoing in the halls. I wanted to believe this was our fresh start, a place where joy could grow like flowers in spring. But sometimes, when I looked around, I noticed the little things that reminded me of our troubles, like dark clouds that refused to go away. Even though I was hopeful, I could feel those shadows lingering, making it hard to fully enjoy the newness of it all.

I couldn't help but notice how little we had. Our furniture was mismatched and worn, and the walls were bare, waiting for the warmth of family photos and colorful drawings. I often glanced at my old, holey shoes and wished for something new, something bright. But deep down, I held onto a tiny spark of hope that maybe this new place would be different. I dreamed of a day when we would have enough—enough to feel comfortable, enough to share laughter over meals without worry, and enough to create a home filled with love and joy. I imagined the possibilities, believing that if we worked hard and stayed together, things could get better, and the shadows would finally fade away.

Our home was small, a tight fit for our family, and while it brought us closer, it also amplified the tension simmering just beneath the surface. Like a chorus of mockingbirds, the neighborhood kids seized every opportunity to tease us. They laughed at the holes in my shoes, which were as big as silver dollars, and I felt myself shrinking under the weight of their taunts. In those moments, I embodied insecurity, struggling with low self-esteem in a world that often dismissed me.

The Quiet Power of Being Seen

Yet, amidst that gloom, a ray of light emerged in the form of Mrs. Gussie Kaufman, my first-grade teacher. To me, she was the epitome of beauty and grace at Douglas Elementary. Her smile was a warm embrace on the coldest days, and her intelligence left me in awe. But what truly set her apart was her ability to see the details in my life—details that others overlooked.

> ***In a world that often glorifies the big and bold, we rarely pause to consider how much of life hinges on the subtle and easily missed.***

Mrs. Kaufman noticed my worn shoes and how I hesitated to join games with the other kids. She celebrated my small victories, praised my handwriting, and offered comforting words when I felt downcast. More than that, she invited me to stay after school to help her, creating a routine that became my lifeline. In a world where I often felt invisible, she made me feel valued. Her attention to the small things ignited a flicker of belief within me, reminding me that I mattered.

One day, she surprised me with a reward: a shiny dime for each afternoon I spent assisting her. Those dimes became more than mere coins; they were my ticket to independence. I could buy candy from the local store without needing to ask my parents for money they didn't have. Each dime was a tangible reminder of my worth, a symbol of my ability to contribute, and a testament to the power of self-belief. In those small moments, Mrs. Kaufman showed me that the little things could change everything.

Then came a moment I would never forget. One afternoon, after the other students had left, I approached Mrs. Kaufman's desk, ready to help as always. To my shock, she opened her bottom drawer and pulled out a pair of vibrant red canvas shoes. They were meant for her niece, but she thought I might like them since they didn't fit. I slipped those shoes on with pride, not caring that they made my handmade dress look even more worn. They were more than just footwear; they were a badge of confidence, a way to express myself, and a reminder that someone noticed my struggles.

Mrs. Kaufman's influence extended far beyond dimes and shoes. She taught me the importance of hard work and the joy of helping others. Her classroom became my sanctuary, a place where love, understanding, and self-worth flourished. The small details she paid attention to—the holes in my shoes, the way I felt overlooked—became the building blocks of my resilience. Inspired by her kindness, I knew I wanted to pass that gift on to others someday.

Sometimes, it isn't the grand gestures that change a life. It's the quiet noticing, the small kindness, the detail that reminds someone they matter.

Despite the challenges ahead, including my journey as a sixteen-year-old pregnant high school dropout, I eventually reached the C-Suite as the only Black female CEO of a comparable healthcare organization in Indiana. I've been honored by two state governors for my work and have been inducted into the Northwest Indiana Business and Industry Hall of Fame. All of this is thanks to Mrs. Kaufman, who taught me that the small things-the details-could change everything and that I was indeed special.

It's about uncovering the hidden forces that shape outcomes, relationships, communities, and destinies.

It Starts Small

In a world that often glorifies the big, the bold, and the obvious, we rarely pause to consider how much of life hinges on the subtle, the quiet, and the easily missed. Yet, it is within these overlooked spaces that transformation happens.

This book is an invitation to slow down and pay attention. It's about uncovering the hidden forces that shape outcomes, relationships, communities, and destinies. From personal choices to professional pivots, from the mechanics of nature to the nuances of leadership, we'll explore how the details—the ones hiding in plain sight—can shift everything.

It's in the Details is a journey to the core of what makes things work, fall apart, or flourish. In the pages ahead, you'll discover that behind every major change is a small, often uncelebrated catalyst. By learning to notice, respect, and act on the details, we open the door to profound and lasting change.

Because life isn't just happening in broad strokes—it's being written line by line, detail by detail.

So, let's begin—not by looking for what is loud and obvious, but by tuning into the quiet power of the details that change everything.

Turn the page, and you'll see: the smallest things aren't small at all; they hold the power to change everything

Behind every major change is a small, often uncelebrated catalyst waiting to be noticed.

This book is an invitation to slow down and pay attention to the quiet power of the details that change everything.

The Quiet Power of What's Often Overlooked

1. **Reflect on Small Moments:** Think back to a time when a seemingly insignificant detail had a profound impact on your life. Describe the situation, what the detail was, and how it influenced your feelings or decisions. How did this experience shape your perspective on the importance of small moments in your life? How can you apply this understanding of small details to your current life or future goals?
2. **Identify Your Catalysts**: Consider areas in your life where you seek transformation or change. What small, overlooked details could serve as catalysts for that change? Write down at least three specific actions or observations you can focus on to create a shift in your current life.

The Power of Small Details

In our fast-paced world, it's easy to overlook the small things that shape our lives. However, research shows that paying attention to details can lead to greater mindfulness, improved relationships, and enhanced decision-making. Here are a few ways to cultivate an appreciation for the small details in your life:

- **Practice Mindfulness:** Take a few moments each day to observe your surroundings. What do you notice that you often overlook?
- **Keep a Gratitude Journal:** Write down three small things each day that you are grateful for. This practice can help shift your focus to the positive details in your life.
- **Engage in Active Listening:** When conversing with others, make a conscious effort to listen to the details of what they are saying. This can deepen your connections and enhance your understanding.
- **Celebrate Small Wins:** Acknowledge and celebrate even the smallest achievements in your life. These moments contribute to your overall journey and growth.

By embracing the power of small details, you can unlock profound insights and transformations in your life.

Final Reflection: The Gift in the Glimpse

Sometimes, the greatest gifts come wrapped in moments so small they almost slip by unnoticed—a teacher's gaze, a coin in a child's hand, a pair of red shoes. These moments don't announce themselves with grandeur; they whisper. But if we are listening—truly listening—they change us.

The story of Mrs. Kaufman isn't just about kindness. It's about attunement—the sacred ability to notice what others overlook. Her attention to the details of my life helped shape the woman I would become. Not through lectures or life-altering events, but through a daily rhythm of compassion, consistency, and care.

This chapter is a reminder that greatness often begins in smallness. It asks us to reconsider what matters most—not the headlines or milestones, but the human touches in between. The details we overlook might be the very things that hold everything together.

As you continue reading, may this reflection stay with you: Transformation doesn't always roar. Sometimes, it simply shows up, quietly, as a pair of red shoes.

The Details Beneath

1. **The Influence of Small Moments on Transformation:** Psychological research emphasizes that small, often overlooked moments can significantly impact personal growth and well-being. Savoring these moments enhances mindfulness and emotional resilience.

2. **The Role of Educators in Shaping Lives:** Educators like Mrs. Kaufman exemplify how attention to individual student needs can foster self-worth and motivation, leading to long-term success.

3. **Symbolism of the Red Canvas Shoes:** The gift of red canvas shoes symbolizes recognition and care, reinforcing the idea that small acts of kindness can profoundly affect a child's self-esteem.

4. **Building Resilience Through Early Experiences:** Early life challenges, when met with support and encouragement, can cultivate resilience and a drive to achieve, as seen in the journey from a modest upbringing to executive leadership.

5. **Mindfulness and Attention to Detail:**
   Practicing mindfulness by focusing on small details can lead to greater appreciation of life's experiences and contribute to overall happiness.

*Further reading and selected references for this chapter are available in the Notes & Sources section at the end of this book.

Small Moments Write the Story of Our Lives

The Wolf and the Bee—Small Actions, Big Impact

"One small shift in the unseen world can set off a thousand visible changes. Never underestimate the quiet beginning of a mighty transformation."
— Dr. Danita Johnson Woods

What if the greatest transformations in your life—the ones that realigned your path, rebalanced your purpose, or renewed your strength—began with something you almost missed?

A conversation that seemed small. A gesture easily overlooked. A decision made in passing.

So often, we look for signs in the thunder when the real shift comes in the flutter of wings.

This chapter explores the hidden power of small changes—not in theory, but in the living systems around us. Nature is full of quiet revolutionaries. Bees that hold up the food chain. Wolves that reshape landscapes. And people like us, whose smallest decisions carry echoes that ripple through families, workplaces, communities, and generations.

The bee and the wolf remind us: You don't have to be loud to leave a legacy.

CHAPTER TWO

The Wolf and the Bee— Small Actions, Big Impact

"Big changes rarely begin with big moments. More often, they start with the flutter of a wing, the pause of a step, or a single, unnoticed choice that sets everything in motion."
— Dr. Danita Johnson Woods

Small Choices, Big Changes

The power of small details is nowhere more evident than in nature itself. Ecosystems—those delicate webs of life where organisms and their environments interact—depend not just on large creatures or sweeping landscapes, but on the tiniest of players. A single bee, small enough to rest on your fingertip, carries the weight of global food security on its fragile wings.

Bees and Global Food Security

Bees are a perfect illustration of how something seemingly minor can change everything. According to the Food and Agriculture Organization of the United Nations, nearly one-third of the world's food production relies on pollinators like bees. Each time a bee moves pollen from flower to flower, it performs a critical task: enabling the reproduction of plants, including countless crops that humans depend on for survival.

The power of small details is nowhere more evident than in nature itself...

From the fragile wings of a bee to the silent footsteps of a wolf, the natural world teaches us: small doesn't mean insignificant.

Beyond the fruits, vegetables, and nuts that flourish thanks to this quiet work, bees also produce treasured resources—honey, beeswax, royal jelly, and even bee venom—that sustain industries and cultures alike. Yet, if these tiny creatures were to disappear, the ripple effect would be catastrophic: a collapse in biodiversity, global food shortages, economic crises, and potential famine.

In ecosystems and in life, the smallest agents often have the greatest influence. The same is true of our choices—small, seemingly inconsequential decisions that, over time, can shift the course of our lives and the world around us.

The Yellowstone Wolf Project

When we think about the delicate balance of nature, it's easy to overlook the small details that can have monumental effects. A powerful example of this is the Yellowstone Wolf Project. In 1920, the federal government made a decision that seemed straightforward: they removed the gray wolf from Yellowstone National Park, aiming to tame the wilderness and ensure the safety of visitors. At the time, no one could foresee how devastating the consequences would be.

Yellowstone Without Wolves

With the wolves gone, the park's largest predator, the elk population, skyrocketed. Without their natural checks and balances, the elk overgrazed vast areas, leading to the destruction of trees and other vegetation. This loss of plant life triggered a cascade of ecological changes. The soil began to erode, and the riverbanks deteriorated, causing further harm to the habitat. As the trees died off, the beaver population plummeted. With no dams to create ponds, fish populations dwindled, and other species that relied on the foliage for food—like rabbits and squirrels—also suffered. The absence of a single species had far-reaching effects, disrupting the park's entire ecosystem.

What may seem minor can alter the trajectory of everything around it.

Wolves Return, Balance Restored

After decades of advocacy and research, wolves were reintroduced to Yellowstone in 1995. The impact was nothing short of remarkable. Almost immediately, the elk population began to decline as they adjusted their grazing habits to avoid areas where wolves hunted. This shift allowed trees and grasslands to flourish once again. With the resurgence of vegetation, various bird species returned, and the riverbanks stabilized, reducing erosion. Beavers came back, rebuilding their dams and creating habitats that benefited fish and other aquatic creatures like otters and muskrats. The reintroduction of the wolves, often regarded as a keystone species, effectively saved the park's collapsing ecosystem.

Balance is restored not by force—but by the quiet return of that which is missing.

As we reflect on the intricate web of life within Yellowstone National Park, it becomes clear that the removal and subsequent reintroduction of the gray wolf serves as a powerful reminder of how details—often overlooked—can have profound implications. The decision to remove the wolves seemed simple, aimed at ensuring visitor safety and controlling wildlife. Yet, the details of this decision—its long-term ecological consequences—were not fully understood at the time. The ripple effects that followed illustrate how a seemingly minor action can lead to significant and far-reaching consequences.

Nature's Lesson: Nothing is Too Small to Matter

In our own lives, we often make choices without considering their potential impact. Whether it's a decision about our health, relationships, or career, the details matter. Each choice, no matter how small, contributes to the larger picture of our existence. Just as the reintroduction of the gray wolf restored balance to the park, mindful attention to the details in our lives can lead to a more harmonious and fulfilling journey.

Every choice we make is part of a larger ecosystem—visible or not.

As we delve deeper into the significance of details, we will explore how recognizing and valuing these small elements can lead to transformative changes in our personal ecosystems and the world around us. The story of the Yellowstone Wolf Project serves as a vivid illustration of how the intricate connections in nature mirror the complexities of our own lives, reminding us that even the smallest details can shape the future in unexpected and profound ways.

From the fragile wings of a bee to the silent footsteps of a wolf, the natural world teaches us a profound lesson: the smallest details, the quietest actions, often hold the greatest influence. Whether it's a pollinator sustaining our global food supply or a predator maintaining the balance of an entire ecosystem, these examples show that what may seem minor can alter the trajectory of everything around it.

The same is true for us. The decisions we make—what we say yes to, what we refuse, how we show up in everyday moments—are like pebbles cast into a pond, sending ripples far beyond what we can see in the moment. Just as Yellowstone's balance hinged on the return of the gray wolf, the harmony and direction of our lives often depend on the small, intentional choices we make.

Nature doesn't overlook the small things.
And neither should we.

As we move forward, we will explore how noticing and acting on the finer details—the seemingly insignificant shifts in mindset, habit, or perspective—can unlock major transformations. Nature, after all, doesn't overlook the small things. And neither should we.

Small Shift, Big Ripple

1. **The Unexpected Impact:** What was one small decision you made recently that had a larger impact than you expected? How did it influence your mood, your relationships, or your productivity?

2. **Habit Ripple Effect**: Is there a habit you've developed—intentionally or not—that's rippling out into other areas of your life? Is it creating clarity or chaos?

3. **Embracing Change:** Now, think of one small shift you could make this week. Maybe it's drinking more water, reaching out to someone you've lost touch with, or changing how you start your day. How do you anticipate this shift will affect your overall well-being?

The Science of the Ripple Effect

Scientists call it a trophic cascade—a phenomenon where a single change in one part of an ecosystem sets off a chain reaction throughout the entire system. When wolves were removed from Yellowstone, it wasn't just about predators and prey. It was about trees, rivers, fish, birds, and even soil.

This concept applies to our personal lives too. A single habit change—like getting more sleep, speaking more kindly to ourselves, or saying "no" to one thing that drains us—can trigger unexpected transformations in our health, relationships, and mindset.

Want to change your world? Start with one small thing you can control.

Final Reflection: The Echo in the Ecosystem

Change doesn't always announce itself with noise. Sometimes, it arrives like a flutter—the flap of a wing, the return of a predator, the smallest shift in a morning routine. Yet these quiet forces often set off a chain reaction that reshapes everything around them.

In nature, we call it balance. In life, we call it alignment. But at its core, it's the same truth: the details matter.

> ***The bee doesn't know it's feeding nations. The wolf doesn't aim to rewild rivers. And we, too, often change the world without even realizing it.***

The bee doesn't know it's feeding nations. The wolf doesn't aim to rewild rivers. And we, too, often make decisions unaware of the echoes they will leave behind. A kind word, a boundary set, a moment of pause instead of reaction—these are not just personal choices. They ripple outward, shifting atmospheres, reshaping environments, and even restoring what was lost.

So, take a moment to ask yourself: What's the wolf you need to reintroduce? What small, consistent choice might restore balance in your life, your home, your work, or your heart?

Sometimes, the most profound impact begins not with what we add, but with what we restore—one small detail at a time.

The Details Beneath

1. **The Butterfly Effect and Chaos Theory:** The "butterfly effect," drawn from chaos theory, illustrates how even the smallest actions or changes—like the flap of a butterfly's

wings—can lead to significant and unforeseen consequences. It underscores the powerful role of detail in shaping larger outcomes. The butterfly effect may be a metaphor, but bees are evidence. Each tiny impact of pollination sets off a chain reaction—nourishing ecosystems, sustaining food supplies, and shaping the world in ways we rarely see.

2. **The Essential Role of Pollinators:** Pollinators like bees are responsible for the reproduction of more than 75% of the world's flowering plants and approximately 35% of global food crops. Their quiet, everyday work reveals how small, often unnoticed actors sustain life and global ecosystems.

*Further reading and selected references for this chapter are available in the Notes & Sources section at the end of this book.

Small Moments Write the Story of Our Lives

Life is a Mosaic—How the Fragments Form the Whole

"Life isn't built in milestones. It's shaped in the spaces between—where quiet choices create lasting legacies."
— Dr. Danita Johnson Woods

We often chase big milestones, thinking they alone will define our lives—graduations, weddings, promotions, or turning points. But ask anyone to describe their most meaningful memories, and they'll likely mention a quiet morning ritual, a spontaneous laugh with a friend, or the silent peace after choosing the harder right over the easier wrong.

These are the moments that build a life—not all at once, but layer by layer.

Life is not sculpted with grand strokes. It is assembled like a mosaic—tile by tile, detail by detail. And just like in art, it is the tiniest pieces that make the bigger picture possible. Some shine. Some crack. Some are nearly invisible. But every one of them belongs.

In this chapter, we pause to notice those moments—to honor the habits, details, and tiny decisions that often go unseen but ultimately shape everything.

Because the foundation of focus isn't found in control or striving—it's found in the sacredness of the small.

CHAPTER THREE

Life is a Mosaic—How the Fragments Form the Whole

"Life isn't made in leaps—it's layered in moments. Each one, no matter how small, belongs."
— Dr. Danita Johnson Woods

Life is not defined by big moments alone. It is a mosaic—a vibrant, ever-evolving picture made up of small choices, quiet experiences, and overlooked details. Each moment, each habit, and each decision is like a tile in that mosaic. Some are bright and joyful, others cracked or imperfect, but all of them matter. They come together to form the story of who we are.

Your life is not built in the big moments—it's built in the spaces in between. From milestones like graduations, marriages, or career shifts, to the quiet in-between moments—a conversation with a friend, the morning coffee ritual, an encouraging text—our lives are composed of details that, when connected, reveal a greater narrative. Even the smallest experiences influence the direction of our journey.

What you do daily is who you become eventually. Neuroscience confirms this: the brain is shaped by what we do regularly. Repetition strengthens neural pathways. In other words, our habits quite literally shape how we think, feel, and function.

Habits form through a loop of cue, routine, and reward. The basal ganglia play a key role in embedding these behaviors, making them automatic over time. Through intentional repetition and mindfulness, the brain can be rewired—a process known as self-directed neuroplasticity.

Life isn't made in leaps—it's layered in moments. Each one, no matter how small, belongs

This means our choices, especially the ones we repeat, are foundational. Like tiny brushstrokes in a large painting, they may not seem meaningful in the moment, but over time, they define the texture and tone of our lives. Whether conscious or automatic, each choice adds dimension to our identity.

Small, achievable steps—what psychologists call "small wins"—help build momentum and fuel long-term transformation. These habits are small by design. They reduce decision fatigue and build confidence. A small habit repeated becomes a powerful legacy.

The mosaic metaphor has also been used in psychology and narrative therapy to describe the integration of life's varied experiences—joys, setbacks, mistakes, and growth—into one meaningful whole. What makes a mosaic beautiful isn't just the vibrant colors, but also the way it holds imperfections. Life, too, gains richness from flaws. Challenges and missteps often add character and depth. They remind us of our resilience and authenticity.

A mosaic is beautiful not because it's perfect, but because it's complete.

How Details Set the Tone for Our Lives

The following routines are simple examples of how details can set the tone for our lives:

- ***Morning Prep:*** Lay out clothes, plan the day, or spend 10 minutes in prayer or meditation.
- ***Time Blocking:*** Dedicate blocks of time for focused work, rest, or creativity.

- ***Lifelong Learning:*** Read an article, listen to a podcast, or take a short course.
- ***Mini-Tidy:*** Spend 10 minutes tidying one area each day.
- ***Weekly Clutter Check:*** Tackle one drawer, one surface, or one inbox.
- ***Evening Reflection:*** Journal about what worked, what didn't, and what matters tomorrow.

These habits are small by design. They reduce decision fatigue and build confidence. Over time, they create structure and space for growth.

The Power of Small Wins

Big goals can feel overwhelming. But breaking them into small, actionable steps helps build momentum. Drink one extra glass of water. Write one paragraph. Spend five minutes walking. Every small action is a step toward the life you want to build. Celebrate these micro-wins. They are not insignificant— they are the foundation.

Celebrate the small wins. That's where transformation begins.

The Ripple Effect

When you pay attention to details, your life becomes more intentional. You feel clearer, more capable, and more connected. And it doesn't stop with you. Others feel your energy, notice your care, and often respond in kind. Small choices inspire others to do the same. That's how transformation begins—one choice, one habit, one moment at a time.

Life isn't found in the grand gesture; it's lived in the details.

Soul Pause

The Quiet Power of What's Often Overlooked

Take 5–10 minutes at the end of your day to reflect on the small details that contribute to your growth and well-being:

1. **Routine Check:** What routines did I keep today, and how did they contribute positively to my day?
2. **Appreciation of the Small:** Did I notice or appreciate something small? What was it, and how did it make me feel?
3. **Lingering Tasks:** Did I handle any lingering tasks that could grow bigger? How might addressing these tasks now prevent future stress?
4. **Mosaic Reflection:** What small "tile" did I lay today that contributed to the bigger picture of who I'm becoming?
5. **Tomorrow's Tile:** If my life is a mosaic, what tile do I want to add tomorrow? Write without judgment, as patterns become clear when we slow down enough to see them.

What small act can I do tomorrow that aligns with the person I'm becoming? Remember: You don't have to finish the picture today. You only need to choose the next tile.

Pausing to acknowledge these details creates space to honor your growth. Life isn't found in the grand gesture; it's lived in the details.

You don't need more time—you need more intention.

Mosaic Effect

The Art and Science of Small Things Coming Together

In art, a mosaic is a composition made from small, individual tiles—some smooth, some jagged, all different in shape and color. Separately, they might seem insignificant. But together, they tell a story, reveal a vision, and express something much greater than the sum of their parts.

Your life works the same way.

Neuroscience shows that the brain forms habits by wiring neurons together through repeated behaviors, small actions that become automatic. These details shape our mindset, our confidence, and even our sense of self-worth. The more intentional the details, the more aligned the outcome.

Want to change your life? Don't look for a giant leap. Look for a single tile you can lay down today.

Mosaic Moments: Your life is made up of tiny, colorful pieces, some smooth, some jagged, all meaningful. Every routine, decision, and emotion are tiles in the mosaic of your story. Take a moment to notice the patterns you're creating. Even imperfect pieces belong. Keep laying the tiles—one moment, one choice, one detail at a time.

Final Reflection: The Mosaic We're Making

We often wait for the grand arrival—the moment that proves we've made it, that all the struggle was worth it. But life, real life, doesn't wait for big gestures. It unfolds quietly. In the in-between. In the unnoticed.

That's the miracle of a mosaic: no single tile reveals the whole picture. But together, those pieces—those quiet, consistent actions—create something enduring and beautiful.

Every ordinary day is a brushstroke on the canvas of your life. Waking up early even when you don't want to. Choosing to be kind when it would be easier not to. Completing a task instead of putting it off. These are not minor choices. They are the fingerprints of focus. The architecture of purpose. The slow-building evidence of a life well-lived.

Even your mistakes have a place. The cracked pieces, the ones you wish you could replace—they don't ruin the mosaic. They enrich it. They make it human.

The beauty of your life isn't in one perfect piece—it's in the mosaic you create from every imperfect one.

So, take heart. You are not behind. You are building—moment by moment, tile by tile, with more beauty than you can yet see.

Because in the end, your legacy won't be one moment. It will be many.

And when the full picture is revealed, it will tell a story worth remembering.

The Details Beneath

1. **How Habits Shape the Brain:** Research from BrainFacts.org explains how neural pathways strengthen through repetition,

illustrating how habits reshape the brain over time. This forms the scientific basis for why intentional routines matter.

2. **The Role of the Basal Ganglia:** The basal ganglia are a group of structures in the brain responsible for storing and initiating automatic behaviors. Once habits become ingrained, this area helps execute them efficiently, freeing the brain for higher-order thinking.

3. **Self-Directed Neuroplasticity:** The emerging field of self-directed neuroplasticity confirms that we can intentionally rewire our brains. Through mindful repetition and conscious choices, new pathways form—empowering transformation at any age.

4. **The Power of Small Wins:** Harvard Business Review highlights how small, consistent victories can fuel personal and professional growth. These "small wins" build momentum, increase motivation, and create psychological resilience.

5. **Reducing Mental Load Through Routine:** Simple, repeated actions reduce decision fatigue and conserve mental energy. This frees up space for emotional regulation, creative thinking, and focus on what matters most.

6. **Life as a Mosaic:** The mosaic metaphor is used in psychology and narrative therapy to describe how life's varied experiences—joyful, painful, and mundane—come together to create a meaningful personal narrative.

*Further reading and selected references for this chapter are available in the Notes & Sources section at the end of this book.

Small Moments Write the Story of Our Lives

Emotional Echoes—The Domino Effect

"Trauma echoes. So does love. The mind remembers not the moments once lived, but the ones repeated with care—or with cruelty."
— Dr. Danita Johnson Woods

We often think of psychology as clinical—diagnoses, studies, and sessions. But at its heart, psychology is the study of how we are shaped, and nothing shapes us more than repetition.

The mind is a pattern-making machine. It remembers rhythms. It absorbs tone. It encodes what it sees over and over again. Whether it's the warmth of a parent's steady hand or the sting of repeated neglect, the brain always takes note. Not just once, but every time it happens.

Most people believe that trauma, transformation, or healing begins in the big moments—the collapse, the confession, the comeback. But neuroscience tells a different story.

It's the daily patterns that form our deepest truths: about safety, about love, about whether we matter.

This chapter explores the psychology of those patterns. How the smallest repeated actions—both loving and harmful—shape our emotional responses, relational habits, and sense of self. Through Tanya's journey, we'll see how one woman's presence and consistency became the quiet antidote to generational pain. Because it's not what happens once that defines us—it's what happens often. And in the details, the dominoes are always falling.

CHAPTER FOUR

Emotional Echoes—The Domino Effect

"The mind remembers the moments that repeat—whether they heal us or harm us."
— Dr. Danita Johnson Woods

We often think of trauma and transformation as singular events—sudden ruptures or revelations. But the truth is, our minds are shaped not by what happens once, but by what happens often. Repeated moments of care or neglect, safety or fear, affirmation or dismissal—these are the building blocks of our emotional foundation. In this chapter, we explore how the smallest interactions can create either fractures or fortresses within us. And how, over time, even quiet compassion can become the loudest echo in a person's life.

How Small Things Shape the Mind

Human behavior is often explained through major milestones—graduations, marriages, losses, and accomplishments. But underneath those landmark moments are the quiet, repeated experiences that truly shape us: the bedtime stories, the comforting hand on the back, the unspoken fears, the silent traumas. It's in these details that our inner world is formed.

Psychologists have long studied how micro-experiences—especially in childhood—leave lasting imprints on the brain. Repeated stress, emotional neglect, or witnessing violence can wire the mind toward hypervigilance, mistrust, and emotional dysregulation. Conversely, small but consistent affirmations—being believed, being nurtured, being seen—can build resilience, emotional intelligence, and a stable sense of self.

These findings are supported by decades of psychological research. Repeated interactions form neural and emotional patterns that shape how we view ourselves and others. Whether it's a consistent bedtime story or repeated emotional neglect, the brain learns to expect, prepare for, and replicate those experiences. Over time, these patterns become our emotional defaults—often carried into adulthood.

The mind remembers the moments that repeat—
whether they heal us or harm us.

In this chapter, we explore what happens when both realities coexist. Tanya's story is one of hardship and heartbreak—but also of persistence, love, and the quiet power of positive reinforcement. It reminds us that while trauma may echo, so does compassion. And in the hands of one determined mother, the details became the difference.

In Her Own Words: Tanya's Story—The Weight We Carry and the Light We Follow

My parents married at just fourteen years old. Children themselves, they stepped into adulthood far too early, and by the time they turned twenty, they had brought six children into the world—though only four survived. Two of my siblings died during childbirth, a quiet but profound loss my parents rarely spoke of, yet one that deeply shaped their lives. It was the first of many wounds.

My grandparents, strict and traditional, insisted that my parents work hard and take full responsibility for their family. So, they did. My father worked long, grueling hours as a mechanic, and my mother clocked in seven days a week at the local grocery store. Still, no matter how exhausted they were, they made time for us. Dinner time was sacred. Church was non-negotiable. They believed in showing up with words and with presence.

Small things made a big difference. My mother read to us at night, mostly assignments from the classes she was taking to further her education. She believed education was a pathway to freedom, and she modeled that belief with every book she opened and every late-night study session at the kitchen table. She taught us to read, sing, and play the piano. Sunday school and church were constant in our lives, offering us rhythm, discipline, and community. We didn't know it then, but those consistent, loving gestures were emotional anchors—reminders that we were seen, valued, and worthy.

But trauma has a way of circling back, even when life seems steady.

Everything changed when my paternal grandmother was killed by a drunk driver. My father unraveled. The grief cracked something inside him. Anger replaced warmth. Control replaced kindness. He became unpredictable, and home became unsafe. My mother, in her quiet strength, packed up our lives and moved us to safety.

Though trauma echoed, so did compassion.

Though she protected us physically, the emotional fractures had already begun to form. We didn't have the words back then, but we were hurting. My brother, especially, acted out—angry, confused, lashing out at a world that no longer made sense. My mother couldn't understand why. She kept trying to pull us back to the values she had always taught: honesty, respect, and kindness. She spoke often to my brother about how to treat others—especially women. She knew he had seen too much. We all had.

She didn't shame us. She believed us.
And that was everything.

And yet, even in her own unraveling, my mother never let go of us. When the chaos of our teen years turned into cycles of addiction, self-destruction, and emotional detachment, she remained steady. She didn't shame us. She didn't deny our pain. When we finally found the courage to speak about the things we had kept hidden—the abuse, the fear, the confusion—she listened. She believed us. And that was everything.

Validation. Empathy. Presence.

It was not a grand act that saved us, it was the steady accumulation of small ones. Her unwavering belief in our goodness, even when we didn't believe in ourselves. Her ability to keep showing up. The consistent voice that reminded us of who we were, and who we could still become.

Eventually, we made our way back—not perfectly, not all at once—but step by step, back to the core values she had planted in us like seeds. Back to the songs, the scriptures, the stories, and the strength that had always been there.

Reflection: Tanya's story reveals how seemingly minor, repeated experiences, especially during childhood, can shape the foundation of our mental and emotional well-being. A kind word. A daily routine. A parent who shows up. These are not small things. They are blueprints.

At the same time, the story shows how the accumulation of unprocessed trauma—whether through violence, loss, or instability—can quietly erode a sense of safety and identity, especially when there is no language or space to process what has happened.

But just as trauma compounds, so does love.

What brought Tanya and her siblings back from the brink was not perfection; it was presence. Small, consistent acts of love, empathy, and belief became lifelines, reconnecting them to the values they had once known. And those small things, repeated with care, changed everything.

The Echo of Empathy

Tanya is now a licensed clinician with a Doctorate in Social Work. Each day, she helps others navigate pain, trauma, and transformation, often holding space for stories that echo her own. Her two sisters also entered the mental health field, using their experiences to support and uplift others. Their brother, who faced his own battles, has since passed away—a profound loss that continues to shape their journey. While their paths were marked by hardship, the roots of resilience planted in their childhood have grown strong, guiding them toward purpose, healing, and self-sufficiency.

Though once overwhelmed and exhausted, their mother became the quiet architect of their recovery, not through perfection but through presence. She listened when it mattered most. She modeled faith, strength, and persistence. She created a home where, despite the storms, there was always a lighthouse in the distance.

Tracing the Echoes

Science tells us that altruism and empathy are contagious. One act of kindness—especially when repeated—can change the emotional climate of a household, a classroom, even a community.

Think back to your childhood. What are some small but consistent actions—positive or negative—that shaped how you see yourself today?

- Who showed up for you, and how?
- What words or experiences stayed with you—either because they healed or because they hurt?
- Are there details you now realize mattered more than you understood at the time?

Now consider this: What are the small things you're doing (or could begin doing) to create ripple effects of healing, encouragement, or empathy in your own relationships?

Researchers call it the "domino effect"—the idea that one person's consistent compassion can spark a chain reaction of goodwill, safety, and hope.

Tanya's story is proof of that. Though pain passed through generations, so did love. Though trauma was present, so was healing. And what began as a mother's small gestures—reading books, insisting on church, believing her children—turned into the lifework of daughters who now light the way for others.

You don't have to be perfect to be powerful. You just have to be consistent.

Yes, it's in the details. The ones that wound—but also the ones that restore.

The Detail Diary: Healing and growth don't always arrive in grand moments. Often, they unfold quietly—in how we're spoken to, how we respond, and what we choose to believe about ourselves. This is your space to notice the emotional details that shape who you are becoming.

The Ripple of Details: Noticing Small Things that Shape Us

1. **Emotional Patterns:** What emotional pattern or reaction have I noticed in myself lately? Where might that response come from? Is it protecting me or limiting me?

2. **Impact of Words:** Was there a moment this week when someone's words or actions lifted or discouraged me? How did that affect my sense of self or behavior?

3. **Models of Resilience:** Who has modeled resilience, kindness, or empathy for me—either recently or in childhood? What small gesture of theirs stayed with me?

4. **Positive Reinforcement:** What is one small way I can offer positive reinforcement to myself or someone else this week? A word, a habit, a boundary, or a moment of presence?

5. **Restorative Details:** Reflect on a detail from your past that has either wounded or restored you. What did you learn from it, and how can you apply that understanding moving forward?

It's the details that wound.
But it's also the details that restore.

You don't have to rewrite the whole story—just start with one sentence of belief.

The Domino Effect in Real Life

The Science Behind One Small Act of Kindness

Research in behavioral science shows that when someone experiences kindness, they are more likely to "pay it forward." It's called prosocial contagion—when empathy, generosity, or moral behavior spreads subtly across relationships and communities.

Here's how it works:

- A kind gesture—being listened to, being supported, being praised—activates the brain's reward centers, making us feel safe and valued.
- That emotional safety inspires mirroring behavior. We unconsciously model what we've received, passing it on to others.
- Over time, these small moments of care can alter relational dynamics, household culture, and even community norms.
- In other words, your presence matters. Your belief in someone matters. Just like Tanya's mother, you don't have to be perfect to be powerful. You just have to be consistent.

Final Reflection: The Quiet Architects of Who We Become

You don't have to be perfect to shape a life—just present enough to echo.

We are not only shaped by what happens to us, but by how often—and how deeply—we are seen in the process.

Tanya's story reminds us that the human mind remembers more than moments—it remembers patterns. It remembers the tone of a parent's voice. The predictability of a bedtime story. The silence after a slammed door. The comfort of being believed.

Psychology gives us language for it: reinforcement, resilience, regulation. But the truth is much simpler. What we experience consistently becomes our emotional blueprint. And while trauma leaves cracks, love—when steady—fills them like gold in broken pottery, making the healing even more beautiful.

The people who shaped us weren't always perfect. But if they were present—if they tried, if they stayed, if they believed in us when we didn't believe in ourselves—then their details became our anchors. Their echoes, our restoration.

You are someone else's echo now.

So, the question becomes: What kind of pattern are you laying down? What small act, done over and over, might be the very thing someone remembers when the world gets loud?

Because just as trauma compounds, so does love.

And that's why the details matter.

The Details Beneath

1. **Repetition and Emotional Memory:** The brain is naturally inclined to remember experiences that repeat. Whether affirming or painful, these moments become encoded in our emotional memory, shaping how we interpret the world and regulate our emotions over time.

2. **The Power of Childhood Micro-Experiences:** Psychological research shows that small, recurring experiences in early childhood—such as consistent nurturing, emotional neglect, or exposure to instability—deeply influence a child's ability to form secure attachments, build trust, and develop healthy behavior patterns.
3. **Neuroplasticity and Emotional Healing**: Even longstanding emotional wounds can be healed. Through repeated experiences of safety, empathy, and validation—especially in therapeutic or caregiving relationships—the brain can rewire itself for resilience and emotional stability.
4. **The Domino Effect of Presence:** One caregiver's consistent belief, compassion, and emotional presence can initiate a powerful ripple effect. That steady support doesn't just impact one person—it can echo through families, communities, and careers, becoming a quiet catalyst for generational healing.

*Further reading and selected references for this chapter are available in the Notes & Sources section at the end of this book.

Small Moments Write the Story of Our Lives

The Power of Small Changes—Unlocking Growth Through Tiny Shifts

"Big breakthroughs often begin with small adjustments—the overlooked hinge, the silent drawer, the one-percent shift that changes everything."
— Dr. Danita Johnson Woods

We often expect change to arrive with fanfare—through grand gestures, bold resolutions, or sweeping overhauls. But real, lasting growth doesn't usually begin that way. It begins with a pause. A closer look. A small adjustment that seems minor in the moment but unlocks a door that had long been stuck.

We don't need to transform everything at once. We just need to notice one thing that's been overlooked.

Small shifts are powerful because they're accessible. They don't require perfection—only awareness. When we take the time to examine the misalignments in our routines, relationships, or mindset, we often find that what seemed broken may only be out of place.

In this chapter, we explore the quiet brilliance of small changes. Not the kind that demand applause, but the kind that restore function, open possibilities, and create momentum. You'll meet Dr. Robert Rohm and his famously stubborn filing cabinet—a story that reminds us that even long-standing frustrations can be resolved with a few focused minutes and a new perspective.

Because often, it's not the size of the shift that matters. It's the willingness to make it.

CHAPTER FIVE

The Power of Small Changes—Unlocking Growth Through Tiny Shifts

Sometimes the key to unlocking major personal growth lies not in grand gestures, but in the details—the small, consistent efforts that accumulate over time.
— Dr. Danita Johnson Woods

In the journey of personal development, we often overlook the profound impact that small, seemingly insignificant actions can have on our lives. It's easy to become overwhelmed by the complexity of our goals and the changes we aspire to make. However, sometimes the key to unlocking major personal growth lies not in grand gestures, but in the details—the small, consistent efforts that accumulate over time.

Consider a common household item that many of us take for granted: a filing cabinet. At first glance, it may seem like just a piece of furniture, but for one individual, it became a symbol of frustration and missed opportunities for years. With a love-hate relationship with a stubborn fourth drawer that refused to cooperate, this person allowed the issue to linger, assuming it was a bigger problem than it truly was. It wasn't until he took a moment to examine the situation closely that he discovered the solution—a simple misalignment that took mere minutes to fix.

This story serves as a powerful reminder that the challenges we face in our personal and professional lives are often not as insurmountable as we perceive them to be. Just like the drawer that had been incorrectly assembled, our habits and routines can be misaligned, leading to unnecessary struggles and delays in our growth. By dedicating time to reflect on our micro-decisions and the details of our daily lives, we can uncover simple solutions that may have eluded us for years.

Let's explore how small, consistent actions create major personal growth, the compounding effects of micro-decisions, and the neuroscience behind making those critical 1% shifts. As we delve into these concepts, I invite you to reflect on your own life. What small changes can you make today that may lead to significant transformations tomorrow?

Let's uncover the details together and take the first steps toward a more fulfilling and productive life.

Reflection: Think about a time when a small change had a significant impact on your life. What was the change, and how did it affect you?

The Power of Perspective: A Lesson from Dr. Robert Rohm

The devil is in the details. A while back, Dr. Robert Rohm was putting some files away in his filing cabinet, a piece of furniture with which he had a love-hate relationship. While the top three drawers opened and shut with ease, the fourth drawer always seemed to be a source of frustration. He struggled to pull it out, and closing it felt like a battle. Despite his best efforts, he resigned himself to using the fourth drawer solely for storage, avoiding it whenever possible.

Recently, Dr. Rohm decided it was time to address the issue with the fourth drawer. After years of tolerating its dysfunction, he moved everything aside and examined the first three drawers to see how they were positioned in the cabinet. To his surprise, when he pulled drawer number four all the way out, the entire rolling track that it sat on came out with it! Everything fell to the floor, revealing that the rolling track had been installed upside down.

Sometimes the key to unlocking major personal growth lies not in grand gestures, but in the details—the small, consistent efforts that accumulate over time.

In that moment, he realized that the reason drawer number four had been so problematic was not because it was broken, but because it was misaligned. With just a simple adjustment, flipping the track over and reseating the drawer, he was able to restore functionality to all four drawers. He felt a surge of pride in solving a problem that had lingered for years, a problem that he had assumed required a much larger solution. "I was so proud of myself, he said!" "I found that I now had a file cabinet that had four drawers that all worked just fine. The problem was drawer number four had been assembled incorrectly."

What struck him most was how long he had allowed this minor inconvenience to affect his daily life. He had mistakenly thought that the issue was too daunting to tackle when all it required was a few minutes of concentrated effort.

This experience taught him a valuable lesson: sometimes, the solutions to our problems are simpler than we think, and it only takes a moment of reflection to uncover them.

Just like the drawer that had been incorrectly assembled, our habits and routines can be misaligned, leading to unnecessary struggles and delays in our growth.

So, he poses a question to you: What small issue is bothering you today? What might require just a few minutes of your attention that could lead to a significant improvement in your life? Often, we let problems linger, believing they are too complex to solve. But just like Dr. Rohm's filing cabinet, the solution might be right in front of us, waiting for us to take a closer look.

Life is too short to be burdened by unresolved issues. By examining the details and making those small adjustments, we can keep the "devil" out of our lives and pave the way for personal growth.

Unlocking Growth Through Small Changes

Dr. Rohm's experience with his filing cabinet reminds us that often, the challenges we face in our lives are not as insurmountable as they appear. By taking the time to examine the details and addressing small issues, we can unlock significant improvements in our daily routines and overall well-being.

Reflection: What minor inconvenience in your life have you been tolerating? How might addressing it lead to greater satisfaction or efficiency?

This story leads us to consider essential concepts that can guide us on our journey of personal development:

1. **The Impact of Small, Consistent Actions:** Just as a minor adjustment in the filing cabinet yielded major relief, small, consistent actions in our lives can lead to profound growth over time. The act of taking five minutes to examine the problematic drawer reflects the importance of small,

consistent actions. It demonstrates how dedicating a little time to addressing an issue can lead to significant improvements in one's daily life.

This can be tied to the idea that personal growth often comes from small, deliberate changes rather than monumental efforts.

The act of taking five minutes to examine the problematic drawer reflects the importance of small, consistent actions.

2. **The Power of Micro-Decisions:** Every day, we make countless micro-decisions that shape our habits and outcomes. Understanding their long-term compounding effect can empower us to make choices that align with our goals. In Dr. Rohm's story, his decision to finally address the issue with drawer number four, after years of neglect, illustrates the concept of micro-decisions. Each day that the drawer was left unaddressed, there was a small choice that compounded over time, leading to frustration. By making the micro-decision to fix it, he experienced a compounding positive effect—having a fully functional filing cabinet.

   Identify three micro-decisions you make daily that could be adjusted for better outcomes. What small changes could you implement?

3. **The Neuroscience of the 1% Shift:** Making small changes may seem trivial, but the neuroscience behind habit formation shows that even a 1% shift can lead to significant

transformations in our lives. The story embodies the principle of making a small adjustment (flipping the track) that resulted in a significant difference in functionality. This can be related to the neuroscience behind habit formation and change, where slight shifts can lead to substantial outcomes over time. The idea that the perceived complexity of a problem can deter action until a simple solution is discovered aligns with how habits are often maintained or changed.

Even a 1% shift can lead to significant transformations in our lives.

4. **Reflect:** Reflect on a habit you'd like to change. What 1% shift can you make today that could lead to a significant transformation over time?
5. **Mindset Shifts:** The realization that the drawer was not broken but rather misassembled reflects a critical mindset shift. It emphasizes the importance of perspective in personal development. Often, we may create mental barriers that prevent us from addressing issues, believing they are more complicated than they are.

As we delve deeper into these concepts, reflect on how you can apply Dr. Rohm's lesson to your own life. What small adjustments can you make today that will set you on the path to greater personal growth and fulfillment?

ß

Soul Pause

Embracing the Power of Small Changes

1. **Examine Small Issues:** Consider a small issue in your life that you have been avoiding. Describe the problem in detail. What steps can you take to address this issue? Identify one specific manageable step you will take today to begin improving the situation.

2. **Micro-Decisions in Daily Life:** Identify three micro-decisions you make daily that could be adjusted for better outcomes. What small changes could you implement to align these decisions with your goals?

3. **The 1% Shift:** Explore a habit you'd like to change. What 1% shift can you make today that could lead to a significant transformation when applied with consistency? How will this small adjustment impact your overall routine?

4. **Celebrating Small Victories:** Think about a recent small victory you achieved. How did it make you feel? How can you acknowledge and celebrate these small wins to reinforce positive behavior in your life?

5. **Reframing Challenges:** When faced with a problem, ask yourself, "What small adjustment can I make to improve this situation?" Reflect on a recent challenge and identify a simple solution that could ease the burden.

Unlocking Growth

Quick Tips for Small Changes

- Start Small: Focus on one tiny change at a time. Whether it's organizing one drawer or dedicating five minutes to a new habit, small steps lead to big results.
- Reflect Regularly: Take time each week to reflect on your micro-decisions. Are they aligning with your goals? Adjust as necessary.
- Celebrate Progress: Acknowledge every small victory. Celebrating your achievements, no matter how minor, reinforces positive behavior.
- Stay Consistent: Consistency is key. Commit to your small changes daily to build momentum and create lasting habits.
- Reframe Challenges: When faced with a problem, ask yourself, "What small adjustment can I make to improve this situation?" Look for simple solutions.

Final Reflection: The Shift That Changes Everything

We often believe transformation requires something dramatic—a bold decision, a sudden breakthrough, a complete reinvention. But more often, the true catalyst for growth is far less visible. It's in the overlooked drawer. The repeated delay. The habit we didn't realize was shaping our day.

Dr. Rohm's story reminds us that the problem isn't always as complicated as it seems. Sometimes it's just misaligned. And the shift we need is not a total overhaul, but a simple adjustment—flipping the track, reframing the problem, doing the one small thing we've been putting off.

That's the quiet brilliance of small changes. They're accessible. Repeatable. Powerful. A one-percent shift might not seem like much today—but repeated over time, it reshapes your life. The key is to notice what's been ignored, and then choose, with intention, to act.

You don't need to fix everything at once. You just need to find the drawer that sticks—and give it your attention.

Because momentum begins with one hinge, one decision, one detail.

And that's the power of small changes.

As you conclude this chapter, consider how even the smallest changes in your daily choices can become a powerful force for lasting change in your life.

The Details Beneath

1. **Alignment and Clarity:** The Filing Cabinet Metaphor: Dr. Robert Rohm's metaphor illustrates how a single misaligned drawer can stop an entire filing cabinet from functioning. In life, small misalignments—unnoticed habits, assumptions, or behaviors—can block our progress until we make a simple, intentional correction.

2. **The Impact of Micro-Decisions:** Research reveals that small, repeated choices—what time we wake up, how we respond to stress, whether we pause before reacting—

gradually shape who we become. These micro-decisions quietly build our habits, self-image, and long-term outcomes.

3. **Rewiring the Brain Through Repetition:** Neuroscience confirms that the brain changes with use. When we repeat even minor behavioral shifts, we strengthen new neural pathways, allowing those changes to become part of our default response over time.

4. **The 1% Improvement Model:** The theory of marginal gains suggests that striving for just 1% improvement in multiple areas can create exponential transformation. Small, sustained changes compound into big results when applied consistently.

5. **The Power of Mindset Shifts:** Often, the first and most powerful shift happens in our thinking. When we reframe a challenge—seeing it as a pattern rather than a flaw, or a signal rather than a stop sign—we open the door to practical, previously hidden solutions.

*Further reading and selected references for this chapter are available in the Notes & Sources section at the end of this book.

Small Moments Write the Story of Our Lives

The Power of Precision—Davion's Journey

"Success doesn't live in noise or speed. It lives in the unseen margin where care, preparation, and precision quietly stack into greatness."
— Dr. Danita Johnson Woods

In a world that often celebrates rapid results and grand gestures, it's easy to overlook the subtle forces that truly drive success. Yet, as we delve deeper into the narratives of those who've achieved remarkable feats, a common thread emerges: the unwavering commitment to precision.

Precision isn't merely about meticulousness; it's about intentionality. It's the deliberate choice to focus on the nuances, to refine processes, and to approach each task with purpose. This chapter explores how such an approach can transform aspirations into tangible achievements.

Enter Davion—a multifaceted individual balancing the roles of student, mentor, coach, and aspiring entrepreneur. Through his journey, we'll witness how embracing precision in every facet of life can lead to profound personal and professional growth.

CHAPTER SIX

The Power of Precision—Davion's Journey

"Success isn't built in the spotlight—it's built in the margins, where precision lives."
— Dr. Danita Johnson Woods

In the landscape of entrepreneurship and personal growth, the mantra "the devil is in the details" often rings true. As we navigate our paths, whether in academics, careers, or personal endeavors, it is easy to become enamored with grand visions and sweeping goals. However, the real magic often lies in the minutiae—the small, seemingly insignificant actions that contribute to our success. This is a lesson that Davion, an aspiring entrepreneur and soon-to-be MBA graduate, has learned through his diverse experiences in school, work, and mentorship.

What truly sets people apart isn't just talent or ambition; it's the details.

Davion's Story: The Difference is in the Details

One thing I've come to realize on my journey—through school, work, coaching, and service—is that what truly sets people apart isn't just talent or ambition; it's the details. The small things that most people overlook: the extra email, the follow-up call, the double-checking before submitting something. This kind of meticulousness is what builds consistency, trust, and long-term success.

As a college student poised to graduate, I've been juggling multiple roles—earning my MBA, mentoring youth through My Brother's Keeper Lake County, organizing college expos, working as a Health Information Analyst, and coaching basketball. Each of these experiences has reinforced the idea that attention to detail is essential for success, particularly in the way I approach coaching.

In basketball, small details often make the difference between winning and losing. Whether it's ensuring proper form during drills, anticipating an opponent's next move, or communicating effectively with the team, the margin for error is razor thin. I've learned that it's not just about the X's and O's of the game; it's about how you prepare for every moment, every practice, and every game. Even a missed rebound or a half-second of hesitation can change the course of a game. This principle applies off the court as well—attention to detail is what helps athletes improve and builds a championship-level team.

I've witnessed firsthand how small mistakes can lead to significant consequences. Whether it was overlooking a crucial detail during a game or miscommunicating with players, those moments forced me to slow down and understand that good intentions mean little without careful execution. Conversely, some of my proudest wins—like seeing students receive over $370,000 in scholarships and watching athletes enhance their skills—came from the small yet meaningful steps of preparation, clear communication, and diligent follow-through.

Good intentions mean little without careful execution.

In basketball, small details often make the difference between winning and losing.

Right now, I'm laying the groundwork for my future. I aspire to own a multi-sport training facility and run a mentorship program that helps kids discover their purpose and chase their dreams. These goals won't materialize overnight—they require a steadfast commitment to detail, effective time management, and a clear vision. That's why I'm focusing on cultivating habits that support these long-term ambitions: staying organized, communicating well with my team, creating efficient systems, and regularly reflecting on my progress.

What I've learned so far is this: success isn't determined by how fast you move, but by how well you prepare. Preparation resides in the details. Every drill you run, every game plan you perfect, every conversation you have—it all matters. In coaching, as in business and life, the difference between success and failure often hinges on the smallest of details.

Reflection: Watching Davion rise above setbacks with laser focus reminded me of what Dr. Dennis Kimbro observed in What Makes the Great Great—that true greatness is rooted in discipline, intentionality, and a deep belief in purpose.

Good intentions mean little without careful execution.

If you want to stand out, take care of the small things.

Because in your career, the difference is in the details.

As we consider Davion's story, it becomes clear that the path to success is not merely paved with ambition and talent but is intricately woven with the threads of attention to detail. In every endeavor, from coaching basketball to pursuing an MBA, the nuances we often overlook can define our trajectory. Davion's commitment to excellence and meticulous planning serves as a reminder that in both life and business, it is the small actions that lead to extraordinary outcomes.

As you embark on your own journey, remember that the details are not just accessories to your goals; they are the foundation upon which your success is built.

Soul Pause

The Precision of Progress: Navigating Success Through Details

1. **Reflect on Your Details:** What small details do you often overlook in your daily routine? How can you start paying more attention to them?
2. **Learning from Mistakes**: Think of a recent mistake you made. What did you learn from it, and how can you apply that lesson to future situations?
3. **Success and Preparation:** Describe a time when thorough preparation led to your success. What specific actions did you take to ensure you were prepared?
4. **Vision for the Future:** What are your long-term goals? Outline the small, detailed steps you can take to achieve them.
5. **Building Habits:** Identify three habits you want to develop that will help you focus on the details in your personal or professional life. How will you implement these habits into your routine?

The Importance of Details in Success

The Power of Precision: Key Takeaways from Davion's Journey

- Attention to Detail: Success often hinges on the small actions that many overlook. Whether it's a follow-up email or double-checking a report, these details can set you apart in any endeavor.
- Lessons from Sports: In basketball, the smallest details can determine the outcome of a game. This principle applies equally in business and life, where preparation and attention to detail can lead to significant improvements.
- Learning from Mistakes: Embrace mistakes as learning portunities. Small errors can highlight areas for growth and remind us that good intentions must be paired with careful execution.
- Building a Vision: Establish clear goals and a vision for your future. Success requires commitment to the details that support your long-term ambitions.
- Habits of Success: Cultivate habits that enhance organization, communication, and reflection. These habits are the building blocks of sustained success.

Davion's journey reminds us that precision is not just about perfection—it's about preparation, presence, and purpose. It's about respecting the process enough to care about the pieces. Whether he's designing a practice drill, organizing an event, or sending a final email to a scholarship committee, he's learned that how you do anything is how you do everything.

In a culture that often celebrates speed, Davion teaches us to celebrate intentionality. Because it's not always the biggest idea that wins—it's the clearest plan, the cleanest execution, and the quiet consistency behind the scenes.

Success doesn't come from hustle alone. It comes from habits. From small systems repeated with excellence. From noticing what others rush past.

Final Reflection: Excellence in the Edges

In every industry, every dream, and every life, excellence hides in the edges. It lives in the spaces where most people stop paying attention. In the email that's proofread one more time. In the practice that runs five minutes longer. In the way you speak to someone when no one is watching.

Davion's story is not just about success—it's about stewardship. Stewardship of time, of talent, and of trust. And the lesson is clear: you don't earn credibility through charisma; you earn it through consistency. Not by being the loudest voice in the room, but by being the most prepared. The most present. The most precise.

You don't earn respect through flash. You earn it through follow-through.

Precision is not perfection—it is presence. A commitment to show up with excellence, even when no one is watching.

Davion's journey reminds us that success doesn't come from hustle alone. It comes from habits. From small systems repeated with excellence. From noticing what others rush past. From honoring the process—especially when no one else is watching.

So, if you want to build something great, don't just dream bigger. Execute better. Care deeper. Slow down enough to notice what matters.

Because in a world that overlooks the details, making them matter is what sets you apart. So, the next time you wonder if the small stuff matters, remember this:

The details aren't just part of the journey. They are the journey.

Make yours count.

You don't need to do more to stand out. You just need to care more about the details."

The Details Beneath

1. **Precision in Practice:** Davion's story illustrates that true excellence isn't accidental—it's built through consistent, careful attention to detail. Whether executing a play or making a leadership decision, small, precise actions are what ultimately define greatness.

2. **Transferable Skills from Sports to Life:** His evolution from athlete to coach and business leader highlights how the discipline, timing, and focus learned in sports can serve as a blueprint for professional and organizational success.

3. **Systems Behind Success:** Every high performer relies on more than talent—intentional habits, clear communication, and structured routines form the hidden architecture that supports visible achievement.

*Further reading and selected references for this chapter are available in the Notes & Sources section at the end of this book.

Small Moments Write the Story of Our Lives

The Subtle Shift—How Small Changes Reclaimed My Life

"The whisper that tells you the truth will always speak louder than the lie that kept you silent."
— Dr. Danita Johnson Woods

How the Quietest Moments Reveal the Loudest Truths

We often anticipate that significant change arrives with fanfare—a dramatic event, a bold decision, a clear turning point. Yet, more often, transformation begins in silence. It's the quiet realization, the subtle shift in perception, the accumulation of overlooked details that gently steer us toward a new path.

In this chapter, we explore how the smallest cues—those tiny, almost imperceptible signs—can ignite profound personal revival. It's a journey through the nuances that, while easily dismissed, hold the power to awaken, heal, and guide us back to ourselves.

CHAPTER SEVEN

The Subtle Shift—How Small Changes Reclaimed My Life

"Freedom doesn't always come with a bang.
Sometimes, it arrives in a whisper you finally believe.
— Dr. Danita Johnson Woods

The Myth of the Big Moment

Most people imagine a toxic relationship ends with a bang—a dramatic argument, a betrayal, a moment so big it can't be ignored. But sometimes, it ends with a whisper. A quiet awakening after years of small things that didn't sit right.

Not bruises. Not slamming doors. Just... silence. Indifference. Confusion. Resentment.

For years, I was married to a man who could light up a room with charm but slowly dimmed the light in mine. It didn't happen all at once. It happened in the details.

It wasn't the storms that wore me down—it was the drought.

The whisper that tells you the truth will always speak louder than the lie that kept you silent.

The Slow Fade

I met him at a buffet restaurant, a place I had never been before. I was there with our company CFO and a group of accountants conducting our organization's audit. At the time, I was the Director of Administration, second only to the CEO.

He approached me at the salad bar. He was pleasant, flirtatious, and appeared confident. I wasn't interested, so I brushed him off. He returned to his seat, where I noticed he was dining with another person, who I later learned was his boss.

Weeks later, we returned—and so did he. This time, he approached again, and we exchanged business cards. He called a few weeks later and asked me to lunch at a local Chinese restaurant.

He told me he was single, had never been married, and had a daughter who was now in college. He said that he had attended college after graduating high school and went on a football scholarship, but left before he received his degree. He wanted to get a job to support his child. His high school girlfriend had become pregnant, and he wanted to be home to help take care of her.

I told him I was divorced with three children. one in college, two at home, and that I was working on my second master's degree. He seemed impressed by my accomplishments. And I had earned everyone. I was stable, successful, and independent.

As we dated, our differences became clear. I owned my home and drove a new car. He lived in a small apartment and drove a city-issued vehicle. He was known around town, charming, talkative, and perfectly at ease in the spotlight. I, on the other hand, was more reserved—quiet, observant, and comfortable in the background. From that vantage point, I often caught glimpses of things others didn't notice. He worked part-time for a local radio station and hosted a community TV show. In public, he enjoyed taking me out, introducing me proudly, and basking in the attention we drew. At first, it felt flattering, but over time, I realized I was less a partner and more a trophy—polished for display. In the moment, our differences felt like balance. Only later did I understand they were the quiet architecture of what was to come. What began as contrast soon became friction. *The very qualities that once drew us together began quietly pulling us apart.* At first, it was nothing I could point to—just a shift in tone, a coolness that settled between us. But little by little, small cracks began to show. Later, I would understand that what I had taken for confidence was something else entirely—narcissism. What I had mistaken for charm was control. Beneath the surface, the cracks widened, revealing fault lines I could no longer ignore. *And soon, those fault lines would shake the very foundation of what we had built.*

At first, the foundation shifted so subtly, I almost convinced myself it was still solid.

The Lies That Followed

One day, a colleague mentioned knowing him from childhood and casually referred to his ex-wife. The revelation caught me off guard—he had always claimed he had never been married, never lived with a wife. When I confronted him about the inconsistency, he admitted to the marriage but quickly minimized its significance. He said he only did it "so the baby would not be born illegitimate." I was unsettled by how easily he dismissed such a significant part of his life, but in the end, I let it go, without realizing it wouldn't be the last truth he'd bend.

Later, when I received a job offer in another city, he proposed. I said yes. Then he revealed he had another daughter from an affair with a married woman. Again, I rationalized. It happened before me, I told myself. I convinced myself I could live with it.

We got married. And that's when the mask began to fall.

Slowly, I began to question myself. If I pointed out something that felt off, he'd say I was overthinking. "You're too sensitive," he'd say. "You always have to be right." My instincts grew quieter under the weight of constant self-doubt.

He downplayed my accomplishments. Dismissed my degrees. Mocked my intelligence. "You think you're so smart." "Nobody likes you—not even your family." And yet in public, he praised me.

He isolated me from people who cared, including his own family members. He never said it outright, but tension brewed whenever I was around my support systems. The message was always clear: he was the only one who truly understood me. Later, I realized that his fear of one of them letting slip some of the secrets he was trying to keep from me played a significant role in this isolation. It also dawned on me that his need to be the center of attention meant he didn't want any focus diverted to me.

He never accepted blame. If there was a problem, it was my fault. Always. And if I expressed hurt, he acted like I was crazy.

Meanwhile, he stopped contributing financially. "You make more money than me," he'd say, as if that was justification to do less. I paid for everything. And I carried more than bills—I carried the weight of pretending we were okay.

What I thought was confidence was narcissism.
What I mistook for charisma was control.

Remembering Who I Am

Eventually, the final truths surfaced. Another child came to light. A denied son that everyone else knew about. A past riddled with lies—he had never been married and never lived with his ex-wife. He left college to get a job and support his child. Another lie. I learned he had been expelled from college for inciting a riot and setting a lab on fire. Everything I thought I knew had been carefully crafted.

Still, I stayed. For far too long.

I stayed because I believed in the sanctity of marriage. I believed I could fix it. I believed in loyalty. But one day, something shifted.

A whisper: "I've got you."

God had been speaking. I had been praying. And when I finally listened, I knew I had to go. I began to make my exit plan. I knew I'd have to pay to be free. And I did.

Rebuilding After the Fall

When I left, the smear campaign started. He tried to ruin my name, my relationships, and my reputation, playing the victim as if I were the one doing terrible things by getting a divorce. Suddenly, it was my fault that he had to move into a two-bedroom apartment—again! My daughter reminded me that he was living in that same two-bedroom apartment when I met him, which made me chuckle. I was essentially sending him back to where I found him! Friends and family called, acquaintances reached out, and they all told me they knew the truth. They shared that they had lost respect for him. The smear campaign didn't work—because the truth stood taller than the lies, and frankly, I didn't feel sorry for him one bit.

What I hadn't anticipated was the extent of his betrayal. He stole from me—valuable jewelry, including expensive diamond pieces that I had bought for myself over the years, and entire rooms of furniture he moved out while I was away. He even engaged his unscrupulous friend to help him steal tools and equipment from our home, all of this occurring before we could even agree upon how to divide our property in the divorce settlement.

Looking back, I realize now—he didn't choose me for love. He only loved himself. He chose me for what I could give him: a stable life, a beautiful home, financial comfort, and status by association. I had the career, the education, the respect. He wanted access to all of it. At the time, I didn't think in those terms. I believed we were building something together, a mutual commitment rooted in love and partnership. But for him, it was transactional. I was the upgrade. I was the opportunity. And for years, I never questioned that dynamic—because I didn't see myself as someone to be taken from. I saw myself as someone to build with.

In the end, he walked away with money. But I walked away with something far more valuable:

Peace. Joy. Freedom.

In the end, he got a payout. I got peace. And I'd choose peace every time.

Love, Reimagined: What Love Taught Me

After years of emotional drought, I never expected to love again—not with ease, not with laughter, not with the joy of being fully seen. But then came Michael.

Michael was a wonderful man. We loved and respected each other. We enjoyed one another's company and never seemed to tire of just being together Whether it was sharing a quiet dinner at home, laughing in the car on a road trip, or having deep conversations about life and faith—we just fit.

Our love was peaceful, grounded, and life-giving. It was thoughtful, not manipulative. There was never competition. No tension. No pretense.

It showed me what safety feels like. What partnership looks like. What love can be when it does not demand that you disappear. We were two whole people simply choosing each other, daily.

With Michael, I was free to be strong. I didn't have to explain or apologize for my ambition, my success, or my voice. He didn't try to silence me, he listened. He supported my dreams. He didn't make me feel like I had to choose between love and self-respect.

Here's what I've learned about love since then:

- **Love doesn't demand that you shrink.** In my past, I was made to feel too "much"—too driven, too accomplished, too independent. But Michael reminded me that those qualities are gifts. He affirmed me in them. He didn't feel threatened, he felt proud.
- **Red flags show up in the details**. They come in subtle control, emotional withdrawal, small lies, and disrespect disguised as jokes. I see them now. I don't excuse them. I name them for what they are.
- **Green flags are everything.** I treasure consistency, kindness, and empathy. Michael checked in with me, not out of obligation, but out of care. He showed up, helped out, and partnered with me in the everyday things. That's love.
- **Love lives in the little things.** It was in how he remembered my favorite foods. How he offered his hand when I was tired. How he looked at me with kindness, even when we disagreed. These weren't grand gestures. They were small, steady signs that I was loved, seen, and safe.

I now know what real love feels like. It didn't confuse me. It didn't drain me. It lifted me. It expanded me.

And most of all, real love let's you rest.

Soul Pause

"God's whispers often begin where your own voice has gone quiet."

Take a moment to breathe deeply.

What whispers have you been ignoring—the quiet truths that tug gently at your heart?

They're not always loud or urgent. Sometimes, God doesn't shout; He simply waits for your stillness.

Close your eyes. Think about one area of your life that has felt uneasy—not broken, just unsettled.

Ask yourself: What is this unease trying to tell me?

The answer might not come as thunder. It may come as peace.

The Psychology of Subtle Change

In psychology, change rarely begins with grand decisions. It starts in micro-moments of awareness—what experts call "cognitive dissonance resolution." When something feels off, your mind quietly registers the gap between what you believe and what you're experiencing. If you ignore it, dissonance grows. If you listen, alignment begins.

Emotional abusers thrive in those small gaps. They manipulate uncertainty until confusion feels like normalcy. Healing, too, begins in the small gaps—when you start choosing truth over tolerance, authenticity over approval, and peace over pretense.

Healing doesn't rush in. It returns, piece by piece, in the details you once dismissed.

Final Reflection

There is a sacred rhythm to restoration. It starts with honesty, moves through surrender, and ends in peace. Leaving that marriage wasn't the end of my story—it was the beginning of remembering who I was before I forgot. If you've ever stayed too long, believed too much, or silenced yourself for love, know this: You can start again. You can start small. And every small step counts. Freedom is not the roar of escape—it's the whisper of return.

The Details Beneath

When I look back, I see that freedom didn't arrive when I left—it began the moment I believed that I could. That belief was born in tiny acts of courage: deleting a text, saying no, telling the truth to myself. Those small acts became the architecture of a new life.

Every transformation is made of micro-decisions. We often glorify the big break, but it's the unseen, consistent choices—the boundaries, prayers, and self-affirmations—that rebuild the soul. The details beneath my revival weren't loud; they were layered. Faith layered over fear. Truth layered over lies. Hope layered over habit. The smallest details don't just tell your story—they rewrite it.

*Further reading and selected references for this chapter are available in the Notes & Sources section at the end of this book.

Business Hinges—The Lines That Hold the Dream

"Dreams are built with passion, but they survive on precision. The small, overlooked lines often carry the weight of the entire future."
— Dr. Danita Johnson Woods

Why Precision Protects the Vision

In leadership, we talk often about vision—about seeing the future before others can. But what we don't talk about enough is what it takes to protect that vision. To anchor it. To keep it from unraveling at the seams.

Big dreams inspire people. But it's the small, quiet details that ensure those dreams endure.

In the rush of purpose-driven work—especially in nonprofit leadership—passion is abundant. But precision? That takes intentionality. It takes discipline to slow down, ask the hard questions, and read between the lines when urgency says "hurry."

This chapter explores one of the most painful lessons I've ever learned in business: that a single overlooked clause can undo years of work and threaten the very heart of your mission. But it's also a chapter about hope—because what we learn from our missteps can sharpen us, strengthen us, and help us lead with greater clarity and care.

Because in the end, it's not just the bold strokes that define your success.

It's the fine lines you choose not to overlook.

CHAPTER EIGHT

Business Hinges—The Lines That Hold the Dream

"Dreams are built in bold strokes—but they survive in the fine lines."
— Dr. Danita Johnson Woods

In the realm of business, many believe that success hinges on strategy, market timing, or raw talent. However, after years of leading in the nonprofit space, I have learned that the most critical factor—the unsung hero of success—is attention to detail. The overlooked clause. The missed meeting. The unasked question. These seemingly minor oversights often become the hinge on which entire futures swing.

In business, details don't just matter—they protect your purpose. Especially when that purpose is rooted in service. Yet, in the hustle and bustle of daily operations, attention to detail often goes unnoticed, overshadowed by more glamorous aspects of business. Big dreams inspire people. But it's the small, quiet details that ensure those dreams endure.

"The difference between something good and something great is attention to detail."
— Charles R. Swindoll

A Hard-Earned Lesson

Let me share how I learned this lesson the hard way.

Whether nonprofit or for-profit, running a business is incredibly challenging and demands tremendous time, energy, and focus—especially if you want it to succeed.

Friends often ask why I chose to work in healthcare, specifically in the nonprofit sector. "You could make so much more money in the for-profit world," they say. And they're not wrong. But for me, it has always been about something more profound. In this space, I find people motivated by purpose—driven by compassion, not compensation. It's about the mission, not the margin.

Still, passion and good intentions alone aren't enough to protect your purpose; you also need precision, attention, and diligence.

Purpose needs more than passion—it needs protection.

The Vision Was Clear

With that purpose and passion in mind, we at Edgewater Health embarked on an ambitious journey to create a $16 million housing unit for the homeless. As CEO, I felt a surge of pride and excitement as we secured the land from the city, envisioning a safe haven for those in need. Our mission was clear: to provide not just shelter, but a supportive community and essential health care services for future residents.

I remember walking the land for the first time—standing in that open space, feeling the wind on my face, and imagining what it would become: a healing sanctuary where hope could take root again. City officials were optimistic, our board was invested, and our team felt the sacredness of the moment. We were about to build something that could change lives.

Big visions are built one detail at a time.

But Then, Reality Hit

Simultaneously, we were in the early stages of implementing a new electronic health record (EHR) system. Unfortunately, the software was not functioning as efficiently as we had hoped, causing delays in billing and severely impacting our revenue stream. As many nonprofits do, we found ourselves stretched thin and on the edge of a financial cliff.

Purpose needs more than passion—it needs protection.

To continue the project, we needed a financial partner to help guarantee the loan. Driven by urgency, we began searching for one. When we found a potential partner, we entered negotiations quickly, compelled by the pressing need for funding.

But, urgency is never an excuse to skip due diligence.

The Detail That Cost Us Almost Everything

Little did I know, this partner came with secret intentions—intentions that would disrupt our vision for the project. Hidden in the fine print of the contract was a clause stating that the managing partner could replace our organization as the provider of behavioral health services at their discretion. I had been so focused on the larger picture that I overlooked this crucial detail.

It was a grave oversight—one that would haunt me for years to come. Caught up in the whirlwind of negotiations and the pressing urgency to secure financing, I assumed that the details regarding our role as the service provider were mere formalities. After all, we were the heart of the project. How could anyone think otherwise?

The Aftermath

The housing unit was built. Residents moved in. For two years, we proudly provided the behavioral health services we had envisioned from the beginning. We had started to make plans to open a primary care clinic in the building. Then, without warning, the managing partner exercised their right to terminate our role. It felt like a slap in the face. We had poured our hearts into this project, only to be cast aside for an outside entity disconnected from the community we had nurtured.

Despite retaining rights to the property, we found ourselves powerless to provide services to the residents we had come to know and care for. The betrayal stung, and the realization that our oversight had led to this outcome was a bitter pill to swallow.

The Lesson

That experience shook me, but it also sharpened me. I learned that passion needs protection. A great mission doesn't exempt you from making great decisions. Even in moments of urgency—especially in moments of urgency—you must pause long enough to see the fine print.

From that day forward, I vowed never to sign another agreement without a thorough legal review and collaborative discussion with my leadership team. I created a checklist of red flags and dealbreakers. I became more skeptical, more curious, and more thorough—not because I lost my optimism, but because I learned to guard it. I learned that while passion and purpose are important, they must be safeguarded with diligence and attention to detail.

That experience changed me. It reminded me that attention to detail is the unsung hero of success. It is often overlooked but profoundly impacts the outcome of our efforts. Passion without precision is vulnerable. A mission without mindfulness can become a cautionary tale. No matter how good your intentions are, success is often determined by what you choose to see—and what you overlook.

A Call to Action

As you turn the page into the next chapter, I invite you to reflect not only on your dreams but on your diligence. The small things—the things that seem minor, mundane, or even tedious—are often the unsung heroes that hold everything else together.

Because no matter the size of your vision, the scope of your ambition, or the depth of your calling—your future will be shaped by the details you choose to honor today. It's easy to assume that good intentions will carry the day. But the truth is, passion without precision is fragile. And purpose, if not protected, can be redirected by those who don't share your heart.

Attention to detail is the unsung hero of success.

I learned the cost of overlooking a single detail—but I also learned the power of learning from that mistake. Today, I lead with sharper eyes, stronger boundaries, and a deeper respect for the fine print.

Because it's not just in the details—it's through the details that your vision survives.

As you chase your vision—whether it's in business, leadership, or life—remember this: success isn't always determined by how big your dream is. Sometimes, it's determined by whether you read the footnotes.

Toolbox: 5 Questions Every Leader Should Ask Before Signing Anything

1. Who benefits most from this deal—and how?
2. What rights or control are we giving up in this agreement?
3. What could this clause mean in the worst-case scenario?
4. Has this contract been reviewed by legal counsel and trusted advisors?
5. Does this agreement align with our mission and values, even under pressure?

Full Circle: The Details Define the Dream

As painful as that experience was, it gave me something unexpected: clarity. *It's in the Details* is no longer just a title—it's a truth I live by.

Big dreams matter. Bold leadership matters. But the small things—the overlooked clauses, the second thoughts, the tiny red flags—they matter just as much.

> ***The small things—the things that seem minor, mundane, or even tedious—are often the things that hold everything else together.***

In the chapters that follow, we'll continue to explore how the foundation of your life is built not only on big ideas, but on the details, you choose to honor. From business to relationships to wellness, the small things are the unsung heroes of your success.

Let's keep walking—one detail at a time.

It's in the details. That phrase is no longer just a catchy title or leadership cliché. For me, it became a core belief. It's the guiding truth behind how I lead, how I serve, and how I protect the mission I've been entrusted with.

As you turn the page into the next chapter, I want to invite you to reflect not only on your dreams, but on your diligence. The small things—the things that seem minor, mundane, or even tedious—are often the things that hold everything else together.

The Mission is in the Margin

What's written in the margins of our lives and leadership? Contracts. Clauses. Hidden assumptions. But also: courage, wisdom, and second chances. This is your space to reflect on how you steward your mission—especially in the moments that require detail, diligence, and discernment.

1. What detail have I overlooked in a past decision that still lingers with me today?

What did I learn—and how has it shaped my leadership?

2. How do I typically respond to pressure or urgency when making decisions?

Do I pause or push forward? What would serve me better?

3. What systems or habits can I build to slow down and protect the mission—even when the stakes are high?

4. Is there a "fine print" area in my life or leadership right now that I need to revisit?

What would it look like to give it your full attention?

The Small Things Speak

Sometimes it's not the thunderclap that changes everything—it's the hush. The unread line in a contract. The unasked question. The assumption that goes unchecked.

We often rush toward outcomes, celebrating momentum and missing meaning.

We celebrate the big wins and overlook the small warnings. But the truth is: what we fail to notice can shape what we ultimately lose.

- Pay attention.
- The details are always speaking.
- Not to slow you down, but to steady your steps.

Final Reflection: Precision Protects the Vision

"Your vision won't fail for lack of passion—it will fail for lack of precision."
— Dr. Danita Johnson Woods

Every leader has a moment they wish they could rewrite—not because they lacked vision, but because they trusted the outcome without inspecting the fine print. I've lived that moment. And it changed me.

In business, it's tempting to assume that passion will carry the mission across the finish line. But passion without precision is like building a bridge without measuring the weight it must carry. You don't notice the flaw until it breaks beneath the pressure.

I learned the hard way that good intentions are not a safety net. The real safeguard is diligence. Discernment. Reading every line. Asking every hard question. Slowing down long enough to protect the dream you prayed for.

Because it's not just about contracts. It's about character. It's about whether we steward the vision with the same care we used to cast it.

You don't need to become cynical to become wise. You just need to respect the details enough to understand that they are where trust is tested, where promises are either kept or compromised.

So, whatever you're building—read the margins. Revisit the clause. Ask the extra question.

Because the difference between being remembered for your mission or your mistake … is often just one overlooked line.

The Details Beneath

1. **Attention to Detail as Strategy:** In business, attention to detail isn't just about being thorough—it's a strategic safeguard. As seen in the housing project case, even one missed clause in a contract can derail an entire vision.

2. **The Real Cost of Oversight:** Small lapses can lead to outsized consequences—from financial loss to reputational harm to mission drift. The chapter underscores how a single overlooked clause allowed a partner to unilaterally alter service provisions, compromising the organization's objectives.

3. **Creating a Culture of Diligence:** Building detail-oriented habits into organizational culture means going beyond individual vigilance. It requires systems for review, open

channels for questioning, and a shared commitment to excellence at every level.

4. **Balancing Passion with Precision:** While passion fuels bold ideas, precision ensures they are executed wisely. Sustainable leadership is found where heart and detail meet—where dreams are built with eyes wide open.
5. **Equipping Leaders with Tools:** Practical tools, like the decision-making checklist offered in this chapter, remind leaders to slow down and ask the right questions before finalizing commitments. Intentionality protects vision.

*Further reading and selected references for this chapter are available in the Notes & Sources section at the end of this book.

The Invisible Architect—Behind Great Leaders

"Every spotlight you admire rests on a scaffolding someone else built—quietly, faithfully, without applause."
— Dr. Danita Johnson Woods

Leadership is often mistaken for the loudest voice in the room or the most visible figure on the stage. But in truth, the weight of vision is rarely carried by one set of hands. Behind every captivating speech, every well-executed strategy, and every breakthrough moment stands someone else—quietly calibrating, preparing, and protecting the dream.

They may never be called out by name. They don't usually make the headlines. But if you look closely at every moment of brilliance, you'll find them. The ones who stayed late. Who caught the typo. Who answered the midnight call. Who made sure the room was set, the message aligned, and the leader ready to rise.

This chapter is for them.

The invisible architects.

The ones who hold the mission steady while someone else carries it forward. The ones whose fingerprints are on every page, even if their name never appears in the credits. Their leadership is not performative—it is quiet, precise, and foundational.

CHAPTER NINE

The Invisible Architect—Behind Great Leaders

"Every great leader you admire was carried, quietly, by someone you don't know."
— Dr. Danita Johnson Woods

I once watched a leader walk into a room—polished, confident, magnetic. The audience stood before he even spoke. He stepped behind the podium, adjusted his notes, and launched into a brilliant speech that drew praise, applause, and press coverage.

But I couldn't stop watching the woman who walked out of the room just before he began.

She was the one who had printed the speech after making last-minute edits. The one who caught the typo in the title. The one who ensured the microphone worked, the lights were angled just right, and the guest list was in order. No one clapped for her. No one asked her name. But without her, his brilliance might have dimmed just a little. His message might have missed the mark.

No one saw her check the sound levels one last time. No one noticed the clipboard tucked under her arm or the quiet glance she gave to the front row to make sure the dignitaries had arrived. But I did. And in that moment, I realized: the applause that followed wasn't just for him. It was for every detail she carried on her shoulders so he wouldn't have to.

That moment never left me.

Because leadership doesn't happen in a vacuum. Greatness isn't a solo act. Behind every headline, every visionary idea, every iconic moment—is someone whose job was to remember the detail that could have been forgotten. Someone who caught the thing others missed. Someone who made sure the dream didn't fall apart on its way to the stage.

This chapter is for them.

The assistants, strategists, schedulers, stylists, speechwriters, and silent operators. The ones who don't sit at the head of the table but keep the table steady. The ones whose names don't appear on the program, but without whom the program wouldn't happen.

The invisible architects.

They are proof that power is not always loud, and leadership is not always front facing. Their precision, patience, and planning are the reason visions survive the chaos. They hold up the scaffolding while others take the stage.

They don't need the spotlight.

But they deserve the light.

The People Who Carried the Vision

Clarence B. Jones: The Pen Behind the Dream

Dr. Martin Luther King Jr. is known for one of the most powerful speeches ever delivered—"I Have a Dream." But few know that it was Clarence B. Jones, King's legal advisor and speechwriter, who helped draft its original framework.

In the days leading up to the March on Washington, King was overwhelmed with commitments. It was Jones who carefully composed an early draft, structuring the legal and moral arguments that would frame King's address. The soaring "dream" section came later, in an unscripted burst of inspiration—but the backbone of the speech, the logic and grounding that gave it shape, came from Jones's quiet, meticulous pen.

"Martin didn't need me to speak truth. He needed me to help shape how it would land."
— Clarence B. Jones

Katherine Johnson: The Hidden Mathematician Who Sent Men to the Moon

While the public praised the bravery of John Glenn, it was Johnson's complex mathematical calculations that ensured he returned safely to Earth. Glenn famously refused to fly until Johnson personally verified the launch coordinates. Her work, buried in back offices and technical ledgers, quite literally launched American history.

"I always liked learning. And I knew the numbers would never lie."
— Katherine Johnson

Valerie Jarrett: The Quiet Strategist in the West Wing

During Barack Obama's presidency, Valerie Jarrett was a senior advisor, but behind closed doors, she was far more. She was a confidante, a strategist, a moral compass. Known as one of the few people who could speak hard truths to the President without fear or filter, Jarrett helped shape the tone and culture of the Obama administration.

"You can't make good decisions without someone who will tell you what you don't want to hear."
— Valerie Jarrett

Tina Knowles-Lawson: The Architect of Beyoncé's Early Excellence

From crafting handmade costumes in the early days of Destiny's Child to insisting on professionalism and humility, Tina instilled discipline long before the spotlight came. She was behind the scenes—handling logistics, protecting her daughter from exploitation, and helping her navigate a ruthless industry without losing herself.

"I protected her, but I also prepared her."
— Tina Knowles-Lawson

The Architect in My Own Story

In my own journey, I've had invisible architects too. One of them is my assistant, Tara Robertson.

Tara keeps me on track, not just by managing my calendar, but by protecting my focus. She handles the bulk of my scheduling, minimizes unnecessary interruptions, and often steps in to resolve issues before they ever reach my desk. She has a gift for anticipating what might pull me away from mission-critical decisions, quietly removing those distractions. Her work may not be visible to others, but I feel the impact every single day.

Because of Tara, I can stay present for global conversations, strategic planning, and the complex leadership calls that require my full attention. She makes it possible for me to lead with clarity because I trust that the details are being carried with care.

She doesn't ask for recognition. But she deserves it—and more.

I still think about her; the woman who left the room before the applause began.

No spotlight. No standing ovation. Just quiet steps, disappearing down a hallway few would ever notice.

But if you look closely at any moment of greatness, you'll find someone like her.

The one who steadies the dream before it takes flight.

The one who catches the small thing before it unravels the big thing.

The believer who serves deeply enough to make a difference without needing to be seen.

Leadership isn't always loud.

Sometimes, it's a hand fixing a microphone.

A voice catching a missing word.

A mind planning for what could go wrong so something beautiful can go right.

Before we move forward, take a breath.

Remember the invisible architects in your own story—the ones who made your light a little brighter.

Honor them.

Honor yourself, if you've ever been one.

As we step into this Soul Pause, may we remember, greatness is a shared story.

Who Holds the Vision with You?

1. Who are the people who support your success behind the scenes?
2. Have you taken time to thank them?
3. Are you someone's invisible architect?
4. What part of your leadership could be stronger with more support?
5. How can you build a culture that values what's done in the margins, not just the spotlight?

Leadership isn't just what people see,
it's what people depend on.

The Detail Keepers

Invisible Architects Show Up In …

- The executive assistant who anticipates the unspoken need
- The stylist who ensures a leader feels confident on stage
- The speechwriter who captures a vision in just the right words

- The operations director who makes a launch look effortless
- The parent who holds the household down so the dream can rise

Ways to Uplift the Detail Workers:

- Give credit in public, not just in private
- Share platforms, not just praise
- Invite their insights—detail people often see what visionaries miss
- Say thank you—and mean it
- The people behind the scenes don't just support the story. They shape it.

Final Reflection: The Hands Behind the Headlines

In every boardroom, backstage, or behind-the-scenes corridor, there is someone quietly making the extraordinary possible.

They don't lead the meeting, but they prepared the materials.

They didn't sign the bill, but they stayed late drafting the policy.

They won't get the standing ovation, but they picked up the phone, managed the crisis, printed the final script, and caught the mistake that saved the day.

These are the invisible architects—people whose strength lies not in taking credit, but in taking care. Their legacy isn't loud, but it is lasting. Because what they build behind the curtain becomes what we all celebrate in the light.

In this chapter, we've seen how some of the most pivotal shifts in history were made possible not by one person, but by many—by those who chose precision over praise, diligence over display, and service over spotlight.

This is why the theme of *It's in the Details* matters so deeply. It reminds us that greatness is rarely a solo act. It's a collaboration—quiet, intentional, often unseen.

So, whether you're the visionary or the one quietly bringing the vision to life, know this: the details are never just the background. They are the blueprint.

And the hands that hold them are history-makers too.

So, as you move through the world, ask yourself—whose greatness are you quietly shaping? And who might be shaping yours? Shine a light. Name them. Honor them. Because the story of greatness is never complete without the hands that held it up.

The Details Beneath

1. **Strategic Voices Behind the Message:** Clarence B. Jones served as legal counsel and strategic advisor to Dr. Martin Luther King Jr., helping to shape critical speeches and messaging—including contributions to the iconic "I Have a Dream" address.

2. **Hidden Figures in Science and History:** Katherine Johnson's precise trajectory calculations were essential to early U.S. space missions. Though her contributions were once overlooked, her story now stands as a symbol of the power of unseen brilliance. Her story became more widely known after being featured in the 2016 film *Hidden Figures.*

3. **Quiet Influence in Political Leadership:** Valerie Jarrett, senior advisor to President Obama, was a trusted confidante

whose behind-the-scenes influence shaped both political strategy and personal support at the highest levels of government.

4. **Guiding a Vision from the Background:** Tina Knowles-Lawson played a pivotal role in Beyoncé's early career—managing, guiding, and protecting her daughter's path while helping shape one of the most influential brands in music today.
5. **The Executive Assistant as Strategic Partner:** Research shows that behind many high-performing leaders are professionals whose emotional intelligence, discretion, and anticipatory thinking are indispensable to organizational success.
6. **Valuing the Invisible Work:** In many institutions, background labor is often undervalued. Leadership scholars emphasize that emotional labor, coordination, and invisible scaffolding are not just supportive, they're essential to lasting excellence.

*Further reading and selected references for this chapter are available in the Notes & Sources section at the end of this book.

Small Moments Write the Story of Our Lives

Vital Signs—
The Habits that Heal

"Your body doesn't ask you to be perfect. It asks you to pay attention, because small acts of care today become the freedom you walk in tomorrow."
— Dr. Danita Johnson Woods

We rarely notice the quiet erosion of our well-being, because it doesn't come with sirens. It arrives softly, tucked into busy days and brushed-off symptoms. A skipped breakfast here. A restless night there. A moment of exhaustion dismissed as "just tired." And over time, what feels normal becomes dangerous.

But just as decline begins in the details, so does care.

This chapter isn't about transformation through intensity. It's about stewardship through intention. About how the smallest acts, drinking more water, moving your body, listening to a whisper of fatigue, shape the quality of our days, even when outcomes remain uncertain. And for me, this lesson became deeply personal when the man I love faced a diagnosis that changed everything.

What follows is our story. Not of perfection, but of presence. Not of grand gestures, but of choosing to care, in the places where attention matters most.

Because your health doesn't ask for drama. It asks for your daily decisions.

Author's Note

Chapter Ten was written during a season of vigilance, hope, and relentless attention to detail. It was revised after loss.

My husband, Michael, passed away after a long and difficult health journey, one marked by advocacy, presence, and love expressed through care. I did not revise this chapter to change its message, but to tell the truth more fully.

The details still matter. Health still matters. Prevention still matters.

But this chapter now carries the added weight of knowing that even when we do everything we can, outcomes are not guaranteed. What remains guaranteed is how faithfully we show up for our bodies, for the people we love, and for the moments entrusted to us.

This chapter is offered in that spirit.

CHAPTER TEN

Vital Signs—The Habits that Heal

"Your body is where your purpose lives.
Treat it like sacred ground."
— Dr. Danita Johnson Woods

Health doesn't unravel in a day. It fades quietly in the background of our lives—one skipped meal, one missed workout, one silent symptom at a time. We lose it in the overlooked moments—in what we dismiss, delay, and downplay. But healing lives there too, in the ordinary, daily choices we make when no one is watching. And too often, we don't recognize what we are losing until it disrupts everything.

Health doesn't unravel in a day.
It fades quietly in the overlooked moments.

I understand that now in a way I never wanted to.

Wellness is built in small, ordinary moments. In what we eat. How we move. How we rest. How we respond to stress. And sometimes, even when we pay attention, even when we do everything right, our bodies still follow a path we cannot fully control.

Before our own choices begin to shape us, our bodies carry the echoes of those who came before. Family history writes its notes quietly, in the rise of blood pressure, in how the body stores sugar, in the narrowing of arteries over time. Hypertension. Diabetes. Heart disease. Certain cancers. These conditions don't always start with us. They move through generations, waiting for the right conditions to awaken.

Yet none of it is final. Our daily choices still matter. They can quiet inherited risks. They can delay progression. They can improve quality of life. They can buy time. And sometimes, they can do all of that—and still not be enough.

This chapter is about reclaiming the moments we do have. About understanding that the little things are never little, even when the outcome is not what we prayed for. I want to begin with a story that changed me forever.

The Moment Everything Shifted: A Health Journey

My husband, Michael, was a man of integrity, discipline, and quiet authority. He stepped into his father's security business at a young age, assuming responsibility early and carrying it with pride. He led with consistency and earned respect not by demand, but by example.

Later, he transitioned into managing multiple furniture stores, where his gift for relationships flourished. He paid attention to people, to process, to presentation. Excellence mattered to him. He was admired not just for what he did, but for how he did it.

Health, however, was the detail that didn't always receive the same attention.

Our journey began less than a year into our marriage when we applied for a life insurance policy. The physical exam that followed led to a denial. That single envelope disrupted our sense of safety and forced a conversation we hadn't expected to have so soon.

A follow-up appointment with his primary care provider confirmed what the exam suggested. His cholesterol levels were dangerously high. Both carotid arteries showed significant blockage. Immediate action was required.

The timing was devastating. We were newly married, still building routines, still imagining a long future. The idea that his life could be shortened by something silent and unseen felt unbearable.

We moved quickly, consulting specialists, securing referrals, doing what needed to be done. A vascular surgeon at a leading medical center reviewed his case and didn't soften the truth. One artery was ninety percent blocked. The other, seventy. Among the worst he had seen in decades.

Two surgeries were planned. One immediately. One a month later.

Watching, Waiting, and Choosing Hope

The first surgery was successful, though recovery was difficult. Michael faced it with resolve. And afterward, he changed. Not superficially, but sincerely.

He began reading about nutrition. Not chasing trends but learning his body. He cooked more. Ate healthier foods. Moved intentionally. Rested with purpose. These weren't habits; they were commitments. Acts of respect toward a body that had warned him just in time.

Then came the second surgery.

What was expected to be another step forward became a long, painful descent into complications. Hospital stays turned into rehabilitation. Rehabilitation turned into months. Months turned into 177 days of vigilance.

For weeks, I slept in his hospital room, sometimes twenty-four hours a day, watching monitors, learning rhythms, advocating, documenting, working remotely with my laptop set up beside his bed. I did not leave. I did not look away. I paid attention to every detail I could control.

And still, Michael died.

There is no sentence that makes that easier to write.

What Healing Taught Me—and What It Could Not Change

Michael's death does not erase what we learned. It sharpens it. Health is not a guarantee. Attention is not a shield. Love is not a cure. And yet, none of those things are wasted.

Healing is not always about recovery. Sometimes it is about dignity. About comfort. About presence. About knowing someone was not alone.

> ***Healing is not always about recovery. Sometimes it is about dignity, presence, and love that stay.***

Michael's journey taught me that prevention matters. That habits matter. That details matter. But it also taught me that control is limited, and grace is essential.

Nurturing Health: The Importance of Daily Choices

Health rarely collapses all at once. It erodes quietly, through ignored symptoms, unmanaged stress, restless nights, and postponed care. Most people don't notice until interruption forces awareness.

In our story, that truth became undeniable.

Michael's stroke risk did not begin with him. His family history carried heart disease, diabetes, hypertension; threads woven long before we met. Genetics set the stage. Lifestyle pulled the curtain.

Heredity is not a sentence, but it is context.

And while lifestyle changes cannot always reverse damage, they can extend life, improve quality, and create moments that matter deeply.

Health is shaped in the details, the small daily choices that either build resilience or accelerate decline.

The Details That Still Matter

Nutrition. Hydration. Movement. Rest. Stress management.

These choices are not guarantees, but they are investments.

Food is not restriction; it is intention.

Water is not basic; it is foundational.

Movement does not need intensity, only consistency.

Rest is not weakness, it is repair.

Stress is not inevitable damage, it is something we can learn to regulate.

I still believe that.

But I now believe something else too.

Healing is not a destination—it is an act of love.

Sometimes healing does not mean survival. Sometimes it means presence. Sometimes it means bearing witness. Sometimes it means knowing you did not abandon the details—even when the outcome broke your heart.

When Love Can't Fix the Outcome

Some seasons teach us the limits of effort.

- You can monitor every sign.
- Advocate at every turn.
- Sleep in the room.
- Pray without ceasing.
- And still lose the person you love.
- That does not mean you failed.
- It means you loved fully.

Final Reflection: The Life You Love Is Still Built in the Details

Michael's life—and his death—taught me that health is not a finish line. It is stewardship. It is attention. It is care offered without certainty.

Your body is not asking for perfection.

It is asking to be honored.

And sometimes, honoring life means honoring grief too.

Wellness is still built in the details, but so is love.

One choice.

One moment.

One act of presence at a time.

Caring for the body teaches us presence. It asks us to pay attention; to patterns, to changes, to what is happening quietly beneath the surface. I learned that attention is not about control; it is about love.

Even when outcomes are not what we hope for, the act of showing up still matters. The care we offer, the habits we model, and the choices we repeat shape more than our health, they shape how fully we live.

Health is not built in dramatic moments. It is formed slowly, through daily decisions made with intention. One choice. One moment. One act of presence at a time.

The life you love is still built in the details.

The Details Beneath

1. **Healing is rarely dramatic—it's built in daily decisions.** It takes shape in quiet choices, long before results are seen or felt. What feels small in the moment is often what makes the greatest difference over time.

2. **What you do consistently matters more than what you do occasionally.** Lasting health is formed through patterns, not moments of motivation. It is the rhythm of your habits—not the intensity of your efforts—that sustains you.

3. **Your body keeps a record of every choice you make.** In time, those choices become the evidence of your well-being. Every action, repeated or neglected, leaves its imprint.

*Further reading and selected references for this chapter are available in the Notes & Sources section at the end of this book.

Small Moments Write the Story of Our Lives

Becoming Tomorrow—Parenting with the End in Mind

We don't raise children—we shape the future through the moments we choose to show up."
— Dr. Danita Johnson Woods

We often think of parenting as a series of milestones—birthdays, report cards, graduations. But in truth, parenting happens in the in-between spaces:

1. In the car rides after tough days.
2. In the unplanned conversations about fairness and fear.
3. In the everyday moments when we choose patience over frustration, and presence over distraction.

We are not just raising children—we are raising future adults.

And the adults they become are shaped not by the grand gestures, but by the consistent details we model, nurture, and repeat.

In this chapter, we explore how intentional parenting—rooted in small moments of resilience, listening, and value-setting—plants seeds that grow into character. Kyla's powerful story reminds us that shaping a life is not about perfection. It's about presence.

Because raising adults begins in the smallest acts of today.

CHAPTER ELEVEN

Becoming Tomorrow—Parenting with the End in Mind

"We raise children in the ordinary. One ride, one prayer, one hard conversation at a time."
— Dr. Danita Johnson Woods

In the journey of parenthood, every moment matters. The small interactions, the lessons taught, and the values instilled in our children lay the foundation for the adults they will become. Much like health, parenting unfolds quietly, shaped less by singular moments and more by what we practice consistently over time. In this chapter, Kyla Parker shares her poignant experiences as a parent, illustrating that there is no universal guide to raising children. Instead, it's about understanding each child as a unique individual and preparing them to navigate a complex world. Her story sheds light on the challenges and triumphs of parenting, particularly in the context of teaching important life lessons about identity, resilience, and social justice.

"What kind of person do I want my child to become?"

The Unique Journey of Parenting

There is no "one size fits all" approach to parenting. When you become a parent, you receive a plethora of unsolicited advice about how to raise your child. However, I have always believed it is more important to truly know your child and adjust your parenting style as they grow. After all, this child is eventually going to grow into an adult. The question I continually ask myself is, "What kind of person do I want my child to become?"

Even if you have more than one child, each one is their own person, with a unique personality and individual way of processing the world. I learned early on that the best thing I could do is teach my child right from wrong and seize every teachable moment to broaden his perspective. As the mother of a child of color, it was imperative for me to teach him how the world would view him—at a much younger age than I had imagined—and how to navigate it safely.

"There is no 'one size fits all' approach to parenting."

Teaching Life Lessons

The hardest lesson I had to teach my son was about racism. He encountered his first experience at the tender age of five. After getting off the school bus, he made it home before erupting into tears the moment he walked through the door. For several minutes, he cried inconsolably. Once he calmed down enough to speak, he told me what had happened. He had tried to befriend another child on the bus, only to be told he couldn't be his friend because he was an "n-word." He didn't understand what that word meant, but he instinctively knew it made him feel terrible.

In that moment, I felt utterly helpless. As a mother, your instinct is to fix the problem. I felt as though I had failed in my duty to keep my child safe. I had raised my son to see the world as filled with rainbows and butterflies—perhaps a little naïve in hindsight—only for him to discover that there were monsters lurking in the shadows. He couldn't comprehend why someone would dislike him for the color of his skin.

Yet, despite this harsh reality, he has always maintained a diverse group of friends, which reassured me that he was learning to be discerning about the individuals he chose to surround himself with.

Facing Racism: A Harsh Reality

This was not his only experience with racism; it was merely the first of many challenges he would face, not only with classmates but also with school officials and others in the community. One particularly terrifying incident involved a white neighbor who decided to call the police on my son and his friend, who happened to be Mexican, as they were walking to the school bus. My son recounted how the neighbor had initially walked alongside them, engaging in conversation as if everything were normal. But then, without warning, the neighbor veered off toward the trash bin while the boys continued to the bus stop. My son's friend, Alex, decided to take a nap on top of the neighbor's car while they waited for the bus. This seemingly innocent act enraged the neighbor, who called the police.

I was in a meeting when my son texted me, "He called the police on us." Confusion, anger, fear, and concern washed over me all at once. I bombarded him with questions: Who? Why? Where are you? What's happening? When I received no response, panic set in, and I began calling him repeatedly.

Later, he told me that when the school bus arrived, they boarded, but the neighbor stood in front of the bus, refusing to move until the police arrived, despite the bus driver's pleas to let the students get to school on time. When the police eventually arrived with two squad cars, they removed my son and his friend from the bus. After a back-and-forth with the neighbor and questioning the boys about where they lived, they let Alex go but proceeded to put my son in the squad car and take him to school. They even walked him in and "explained" the situation to the office staff as told to me by the police officer after he dropped him off

> ***"This incident made my son appear to be a criminal, potentially leading the staff and teachers to label him as a troublemaker."***

Navigating Difficult Situations

This incident upset me for several reasons. First, it made my son appear to be a criminal, potentially leading the staff and teachers to label him as a troublemaker. I also worried about how much information was collected on him and whether his name would be in their database, used against him for any future offense, regardless of how minor.

I had always taught my son not to answer personal questions and to ask adults to call his mom. Yet, I also instilled in him the importance of respecting adults and authority figures. His honesty, while admirable, often put him in difficult situations. I believe the conflicting messages made it challenging for him. He tended to comply and answer any invasive questions posed to him. As a result of these incidents, he developed a disdain for riding the bus and would often purposely miss it so that I would have to take him to school. Even as a young adult, he still tends to avoid uncomfortable situations, and I strive to encourage him to confront those challenges.

The Ongoing Journey of Growth

When I was able to speak with my son, I told him the police officer had given me his account of the events, but I wanted to hear his. After hearing his side and recognizing no significant differences we had a conversation that was tender but firm, rooted in the desire to protect and empower him, while preparing him for a world that may not always see him clearly or treat him justly. I reiterated that as a minor he should always ask for a parent to be present when being questioned. When discussing police interactions, particularly as he started to approach driving age, I stressed the importance of safety and self-control. I advised him to stay calm, be respectful, keep his hands visible, and avoid sudden movements—regardless of whether he feels the situation is fair. I reminded him that the goal is to make it home safely, and any injustices can be addressed later with support.

I realize now that parenting is a never-ending journey. I continue to learn and adapt every day. I am proud of the young man my son has become. I raised him to be an independent thinker, to be curious about the world around him, and to challenge the status quo. He is an intellectual who enjoys engaging in healthy debates, eager to learn and teach others. I remind him that he still has much to learn, as his brain will continue to develop until he turns 25.

"I continue to learn and adapt every day."

Modeling Behavior

Children are keen observers and often learn by imitating the adults around them. When parents model positive behaviors—such as kindness, empathy, and respect—children are more likely to internalize these traits. For instance, if a parent demonstrates good communication skills by engaging in respectful conversations, a child learns the importance of dialogue and how to express themselves effectively. Positive modeling can also include how parents handle adversity, demonstrating resilience and problem-solving skills. These small, everyday actions create a framework for children, influencing how they interact with others and handle challenges as they grow.

Listening:

Active listening is a fundamental aspect of intentional parenting. When parents take the time to listen to their children—validating their feelings and experiences—it fosters a sense of trust and security. This attentiveness encourages open communication, allowing children to express their thoughts and emotions without fear of judgment. For example, when a child shares their experiences at school, whether positive or negative, a parent who listens attentively can provide guidance and support. This practice not only strengthens the parent-child bond but also teaches children the importance of listening to others, nurturing their ability to be empathetic and understanding individuals.

Instilling Values:

Values are the guiding principles that shape a child's character and decision-making throughout their lives. Intentional parenting involves explicitly discussing values such as honesty, integrity, compassion, and respect for diversity. This can be done through conversations, storytelling, or real-life examples. For instance, discussing the implications of kindness in daily interactions or the importance of standing up against injustice can help children develop a moral compass. The details of how these values are communicated—through family traditions, community involvement, or personal anecdotes—can leave a lasting impact on a child's worldview, influencing how they treat others and navigate complex social situations.

The Bigger Picture

The details of intentional parenting are woven into the fabric of everyday life. Each small interaction, whether it's a conversation at the dinner table, a moment of comfort during a tough day, or a lesson learned from a mistake, contributes to a child's development. These details are not just isolated events; they accumulate over time, shaping a child's identity, beliefs, and behaviors.

As a parent, identify and highlight specific examples of how you practiced these elements of intentional parenting with your child. For instance, you could reflect on moments when you modeled resilience in the face of challenges, listened to your child during difficult conversations about race, or instilled values by discussing the importance of empathy and respect for others. By illustrating these details through personal anecdotes, you reinforce the idea that parenting is an intricate tapestry of small, meaningful actions that collectively shape a child's future.

Intentional Parenting: Nurturing Future Adults

As you embark on the journey of raising your child into a thoughtful, resilient adult, take a moment to reflect on the following questions:

1. **Modeling Growth:** Recall a recent instance where you demonstrated a behavior you wish to see in your child. What specific actions did you take, and how do you believe

they influenced your child's understanding of that behavior? Write about this experience and any lessons learned.

2. **Listening for Connection:** Think about a time when you truly listened to your child. What insights did they share, and how did that conversation strengthen your bond? How can you enhance your listening skills to foster deeper connections?

3. **Values in Action:** Identify one core value that you aspire to instill in your child as they grow into adulthood. What steps will you take to embody and communicate this value through your daily interactions? Write down concrete examples or situations where you can reinforce this value in your family life.

Set aside some dedicated time to explore these questions in your journal. Embrace the opportunity to reflect on your intentional parenting journey, recognizing that each moment contributes to the future you envision for your child.

The Power of Intentional Parenting

Intentional parenting is about being mindful of the small moments that shape your child's future. Here are some key takeaways to remember:

- **Modeling Behavior:** Children learn by observing. Be the example you want your child to follow.

- **Active Listening:** Create a safe space for your children to express themselves. Listening fosters trust and open communication.
- **Instilling Values:** Discuss and demonstrate the values you wish to impart. Consistency in your actions reinforces these lessons.

Remember, parenting is a journey filled with opportunities for growth—for both you and your child. Embrace the details, and you'll create lasting memories and impactful lessons along the way.

Final Reflection: Planting and Nurturing Seeds of Adulthood

Kyla's story offers a heartfelt reminder that parenting is not a destination—it is a continual unfolding of growth, reflection, and resilience. Her experiences navigating race, identity, and safety while raising her son reveal the invisible labor and emotional courage that intentional parenting requires. But more importantly, they reveal the extraordinary power of ordinary moments.

It is in these everyday interactions—teaching right from wrong, listening without judgment, modeling strength in adversity—that the fabric of a child's character is quietly woven. Over time, those seemingly small moments become the bedrock of future decision-making, empathy, and self-worth.

By raising a child to question, to care, and to stand tall in a complicated world, Kyla reminds us that the details of parenting are never wasted. They are seeds. And with time, those seeds grow into the kind of adults this world desperately needs—curious, grounded, compassionate, and courageous. Long after our hands are no longer guiding them, what we planted still speaks.

The Details Beneath

1. **The Power of Everyday Interactions:** Parenting happens in the quiet, repeated moments—affirming a child's voice, setting clear boundaries, and showing up consistently. These daily choices form the foundation of character, confidence, and resilience.

2. **Modeling Over Instruction:** Children internalize what they see more than what they're told. Studies show that kids mirror the emotional habits and behaviors of the adults around them, shaping their sense of morality, identity, and interpersonal skills.

3. **Listening as Leadership:** Active listening deepens the parent-child bond and builds trust. It also encourages emotional awareness and open communication—traits that support lifelong mental health and self-expression.

4. **Parenting Beyond Childhood:** Adolescent brains are still under construction. With executive functioning still developing into the mid-20s, ongoing parental presence and guidance remain vital—even when they appear to need it less.

5. **Raising Children of Color with Intentionality:** For children of color, parenting often includes teaching how to navigate bias, build pride in their identity, and stay safe in unequal systems. Instilling cultural affirmation and psychological safety is both a necessity and a gift.

*Further reading and selected references for this chapter are available in the Notes & Sources section at the end of this book.

Small Moments Write the Story of Our Lives

Composing Clarity— The Discipline of Creativity

"When inspiration slows down enough to become intention, creativity thrives.
— Dr. Danita Johnson Woods

In a world that celebrates hustle, noise, and bold declarations, we often forget where true magic happens: in the quiet spaces. Real creativity—the kind that lingers, moves, and transforms—rarely arrives in a flurry of chaos. It emerges when we slow down enough to notice. In the pause before the brushstroke. In the breath before the word. In the stillness that carries more weight than action.

This chapter invites us to reconsider what makes art, leadership, and connection powerful. It's not just the grand gestures—it's the subtle choices, the hidden moments, the unseen precision. Because whether we're creating, leading, or loving, it's the details we attend to—or overlook—that ultimately shape everything.

Before we explore Mark Spencer's unforgettable stories, take a breath. Lean into the stillness. Because in creativity, as in life, the most important movements often happen in the spaces in between.

CHAPTER TWELVE

Composing Clarity—The Discipline of Creativity

"Creativity begins in the pause—where instinct meets intention, and silence becomes the brushstroke."
— Dr. Danita Johnson Woods

Creativity is often imagined as wild, boundless, and instinctive. We picture paint flying across canvas, melodies erupting from spontaneous jam sessions, or actors delivering lines with raw emotion. But in truth, the most moving art—the kind that lingers in the soul—emerges not just from inspiration, but from intention. It's not the brushstroke alone, but the angle of the wrist. Not the line delivered, but the breath taken before it. The magic isn't in the masterpiece—it's in the moments that build toward it.

Art, like life, is shaped by attention to detail. In design, it's the negative space that brings balance. In music, the rest between notes adds weight. And in theater, as Mark Spencer reminds us, the real difference isn't always in the script—it's in the silence, the glance, the pause.

Art, like life, is shaped by attention to detail.

Mark Spencer, the founder and director of the Mark Spencer West Side Theatre Guild and a master of his craft, shared two stories that embody this truth. These aren't just anecdotes about performance, they are life lessons about the transformative power of subtlety. They emphasize how micro-moments, subtle gestures, and seemingly minor choices create a ripple effect that elevates not just performances, but human connection and meaning. They remind us that in creativity, as in leadership and love, the details always matter.

> ***"It wasn't the words that moved the room—it was the breath she took before speaking them."***

Story 1: The Moment That Made the Difference

I've always believed that the difference between good and great lies in the smallest of details. You can have the best actors, the best script, the most elaborate set design—but if the little things aren't right, the magic never quite happens.

I remember working with a young student—a gifted performer, full of raw talent—but something was off. We were preparing for a major production, and I knew she had the potential to steal the show. But every time she delivered her monologue, it felt rehearsed. Too polished. The words were right, but the emotion didn't land.

One evening during rehearsal, I watched her closely. She paced before her cue, brow furrowed, whispering the lines to herself. When the moment came, she walked to center stage, took a breath, and spoke. It was... fine. The audience would have clapped. But I knew she was capable of more.

"Hold it," I called from the darkened seats. "Start again. But this time, before you say a word, just be in the moment. Don't rush to the line. Let the silence fill the space. Think about what the character is feeling before she speaks."

She exhaled sharply, nodded, and tried again. This time, she didn't immediately launch into her speech. She stood there—shoulders tense, eyes scanning the imaginary space around her. And then—just a flicker of hesitation, a slight shift in posture—before she finally spoke.

That was it. That was the moment that everything changed.

By the time she finished, the room was silent. I could see the difference in the way the other students looked at her. They felt something. And I knew she felt it too.

That night, she discovered what all great performers must find: the power of the pause, the weight of a breath, the electricity of stillness before action. It wasn't a big change. It wasn't a rewrite of the scene or some grand, sweeping adjustment. It was a single, microscopic detail.

And yet, it made all the difference.

I've seen this play out time and time again—not just in the theater, but in leadership, in community work, in life. Sometimes success isn't about the loudest voice in the room, the biggest action, or the most obvious choice. It's about the details—the quiet moments that no one expects but everyone remembers.

And when you learn to see those moments, when you train yourself to find them, that's when the real magic happens.

"It wasn't the words that moved the room—it was the breath she took before speaking them."

Reflection: We often underestimate the power of a pause—not just on stage, but in life. In leadership, in parenting, in partnership, it's not always what we say or do, but how present we are in the moment before we act. That sliver of awareness, that space to breathe and feel, changes the energy. It creates connection. Like the young actress discovering her presence before her monologue, we, too, find our depth in the details we're tempted to rush past. Slow down. The magic is hiding there.

Story 2: The Look That Changed Everything

Rehearsals were running long, and I could see the exhaustion settling in. Devin, one of my most promising young actors, was struggling through a pivotal scene. It wasn't that he didn't know the lines—he had memorized them perfectly. It wasn't that he lacked talent—his instincts were sharp. But something was missing.

I sat back in my chair, watching him move through the scene again. He delivered the dialogue, hit his marks, even gestured at the right moments. And yet… nothing. The audience wouldn't feel it.

"Stop," I called out, rubbing my temples. "Devin, what's your character thinking before he speaks?"

Devin blinked, confused. "Well, he's… upset?"

"No," I said. "He's devastated. But he can't show it. So, what does he do? He looks away. He swallows hard. His hands tighten, just for a second. Then he speaks."

> ***"Great performances aren't built on noise. They live in the silence between the lines."***

Devin frowned, considering. "You mean… I don't just say the line?"

"Exactly. You let the audience see the thought before the words come. It's in the details, Devin. The right pause, the right glance, the right breath—those are the moments that turn a performance into something unforgettable."

He nodded slowly. "Let me try again."

This time, before he spoke, he let his eyes flicker downward. His lips pressed together in the briefest hesitation. And when he finally said the line, it wasn't just words. It was a revelation.

Suddenly, the scene worked.

It wasn't the script that changed. It wasn't the set or the lighting. It was a look—a single, fleeting detail—that transformed an ordinary moment into something powerful.

Great performances aren't built on noise. They live in the silence between the lines.

The difference was in the details. It always is.

Mark's Final Thought: What struck me most about Devin's moment wasn't just his growth as an actor—it was the reminder that authenticity often shows up in the smallest gestures. A glance. A breath. A hesitation. That's where truth lives. We are trained to perform in so many areas of our lives, but it's the subtle, honest moments that truly move people. Whether you're giving a keynote, leading a team, or simply sitting with someone in their pain, never forget: the look, the pause, the intention—they change everything.

Reflection: Creativity is not just a gift—it's a practice of noticing. Whether it's a pause on stage, the precision of a brushstroke, or the murmur of intuition that guides a decision, artistry lives in the details. And so does excellence. The most unforgettable moments—on canvas, in conversation, or in community—rarely come from grand gestures. They come from people who are willing to see what others overlook, to feel what others rush past, and to move with intention.

That's the heartbeat of creativity. That's the difference between doing something and making it matter.

Side Note: The Soul of Stillness

Artistry is not always loud or showy. Sometimes, the most powerful moments are the quietest—the inhale before the answer, the glance before the truth, the stillness before the breakthrough.

These moments are easy to miss, but when noticed, they carry the full weight of meaning. In your own life, are you making room for the pause? Are you allowing the details to speak?

The Quiet Shift

Think of a time when a small gesture—a glance, a breath, a pause—shifted everything. What made it powerful?

This week, choose to move with sacred slowness.

- Pause before you speak.
- Notice before you act.
- Feel before you decide.

At day's end, reflect:

- What did I notice that I usually miss?
- How did stillness shape my creativity, clarity, or connection?

The smallest details often carry the greatest meaning. Let them speak.

Creativity isn't chaos—it's intention, held gently.

Micro-Moments That Move Us

The Anatomy of a Detail

In theater, these are called beats—those brief, intentional pauses between dialogue that reveal more than words ever could. In film, they're the lingering close-ups. In life, they're the knowing glance between friends, the held breath before saying "I'm sorry," or the soft exhale after hearing "I'm proud of you."

Great creatives, like great leaders, don't just perform—they notice. They tune in. They feel the shift in the room, the drop in tone, the flicker of doubt behind the eyes. That's where change lives.

Want to elevate your leadership, your artistry, or your relationships? Start by mastering these micro-moments:

- The pause before you reply.
- The expression behind someone's silence.
- The subtle cue in a teammate's body language.
- The emotion in your own breath before you speak.

Tiny Truth: You don't have to shout to be powerful.
You just have to be present.

Final Reflection: Let the Moment Carry You

Creativity is not just about bold colors or loud declarations. It's about precision. Presence. The breath before the brushstroke. The glance before the word. The decision to slow down and let the moment speak.

Whether we're on a stage, leading a meeting, or loving someone through a hard time, the impact isn't in how loud we are, it's in how closely we're paying attention. That's where beauty lives. That's where meaning takes root.

If you want your work to matter—your art, your leadership, your love—start by noticing what others miss. Then move from that place. The details will carry you.

The Details Beneath

1. **Stillness as the Source of Creativity:** Creativity often emerges not in the noise, but in the pause before it. Stillness allows space for intention, breath, and clarity—reminding us that the moment before the action often carries the most emotional power.

2. **Theatrical "Beats" and Emotional Precision:** In theater, a "beat" is a pause that signals an emotional shift. This concept applies beyond the stage—to leadership, communication, and relationships—where awareness interrupts autopilot and invites presence.

3. **Negative Space as Creative Tension**: In art, music, and storytelling, the space between things—the silence, the rest, the blank canvas—holds meaning. Absence creates depth. Resonance lives in the tension between what is said and what is left unsaid.

4. **The Weight of Subtlety:** The smallest gestures—a glance, a tilt of the head, a breath—often carry the most truth. Whether on stage or in real life, subtlety reveals more than spectacle.

5. **Creativity as Daily Discipline:** Inspiration may strike in a moment, but mastery is built in repetition. Great creators don't just wait for clarity—they train for it. They rehearse, refine, and choose presence as a habit.

*Further reading and selected references for this chapter are available in the Notes & Sources section at the end of this book.

Small Moments Write the Story of Our Lives

One Letter at a Time: The Map to Human Connection

"Understanding people isn't about memorizing traits,
it's about noticing patterns, listening closely,
and learning to see beyond your own lens."
— Dr. Danita Johnson Woods

We all want to be understood. But too often, we assume people think like we do, communicate like we do, or prioritize what we prioritize. And when they don't, frustration sets in—and sometimes, costly mistakes follow.

That's where the power of behavioral insight comes in.

This chapter isn't just about personality profiles. It's about compassion. It's about learning to lead, listen, and love with intention, not assumption. DISC gave me language, but real-world experience taught me how to apply it with humility, precision, and grace. In both leadership and marriage, that clarity changed everything.

Because the way forward isn't found in controlling others. It's found in understanding them.

And understanding? That lives in the details.

CHAPTER THIRTEEN

One Letter at a Time— The Map to Human Connection

"The difference isn't in how people act—it's in how you interpret it. And like most things in life, it all comes down to paying attention to the details."
— Dr. Danita Johnson Woods

We all communicate. We all lead in some way. But not all of us do it well—because so often, we assume others operate from the same wiring we do. We misread confidence as arrogance. Quiet as indifference. Detail-orientation as nitpicking. And when those assumptions go unchecked, relationships unravel and leadership falters.

DISC helped me reframe those assumptions. It taught me to translate behavior, not just react to it—to lead with greater clarity, to love with deeper understanding, and to listen with less judgment.

This chapter is about more than a framework. It's about what happens when we slow down enough to notice how people show up—and begin responding to who they are, not just how they behave.

Understanding people isn't about memorizing traits— it's about noticing patterns, listening closely, and learning to see beyond your own lens.

Understanding DISC: A Map to Behavior

Before we can apply DISC in real life, we need to understand what each letter represents. It's not about putting people in boxes. It's about learning to recognize behavioral patterns that help us connect, communicate, and collaborate more effectively.

The DISC model isn't about labels. It's about observation. It helps us understand how people approach problems, communicate, and handle pressure.

D | Dominance | Results, control | Direct, confident, assertive

I | Influence | People, enthusiasm | Optimistic, outgoing, expressive

S | Steadiness | Stability, loyalty | Calm, patient, supportive

C | Conscientiousness | Accuracy, logic | Analytical, detailed, cautious

DISC in Real Life: What We Miss When We Don't Pay Attention

- Mistake a High C's accuracy for pickiness
- Misread a High I's energy as flightiness
- Dismiss a High S's calm as lack of ambition
- Feel bulldozed by a High D focused on results

Once I understood the patterns, I could begin adjusting my leadership style in meaningful ways. These weren't major overhauls, just intentional shifts rooted in awareness. And those small adjustments made all the difference.

Understanding someone's communication style is an act of compassion, not control.

Leadership: Details that Build Trust

- My emails became shorter for High Ds, warmer for High Is.
- I gave High Cs more context, High Ss more notice.
- I stopped expecting people to process like I do—and valued their strengths instead.

DISC doesn't change who people are—it changes how we see them.

Real-World Impact: When Style Overpowers Structure

DISC has shown me just how much personality styles shape outcomes. When we align responsibilities with those styles, things flourish. But when we overlook them? That's when things go sideways.

Take Audrey, our former Marketing Director. She was a textbook D: direct, assertive, and confident. She loved taking charge—but often failed to follow through on the small but essential details. Many on the leadership team found her abrasive. To them, she seemed bossy, dismissive, even negative. But to her, she was just getting things done.

When it came time for an important accreditation site visit, Audrey insisted on taking the lead. She said she'd done it before and knew exactly what to do. I allowed it.

On the day of the site visit, the accreditation team arrived and we weren't ready. She had completely forgotten the scheduled date and had failed to notify or prepare the staff. People were caught off guard, scrambling to respond. I was humiliated. But our team, as they so often do, stepped up. And, despite the lack of preparation, we had a solid visit and ultimately passed.

Lesson learned? Trust—but verify. Especially with high-D leaders. Confidence is not a substitute for detail.

That wasn't the only costly misstep. Later, Audrey led the development of a $500,000 grant proposal that focused on nursing interventions. She partnered with Melissa, our Director of Nursing, a warm, service-minded S personality—nurturing, agreeable, and deeply competent, but non-confrontational. The two formed part of a cross-functional team working on the application.

When it came time to submit the grant, we hit a major snag—we weren't properly registered on the granting agency's online submission portal. The deadline was that same day at 5:00 PM. There was no time to fix the issue electronically.

At 1:00 PM Central time, Audrey proposed a workaround: have Melissa drive a hard copy of the application 150 miles to Indianapolis. Audrey was confident Melissa could make it if she left right away. But she failed to factor in a key detail—Indianapolis is on Eastern Time, and we're on Central Time. That meant we'd lose an hour.

Melissa made the trip. But between the time zone shift and traffic, she arrived just five minutes past the deadline. The application was rejected.

Melissa returned heartbroken, feeling like she had failed. But she hadn't. The failure was in the planning and leadership. The D personality charged ahead. The S personality avoided confrontation. And no one double-checked the operational details.

That day, we lost a half-million-dollar opportunity because personalities weren't aligned with roles—and details were ignored.

Style without structure creates risk. Strengths misapplied become liabilities.

From Leadership to Love

That same year, I realized DISC wasn't just useful at work—it was lifesaving at home.

Michael and I are both thoughtful and principled. We share a love of logic and value clear thinking. But how we express that couldn't be more different. I'm a C-D—structured, detail-driven, and decisive. Michael is a C-I—thoughtful like me, but more relational, expressive, and people-oriented.

Style without structure creates risk.
Strengths misapplied become liabilities.

Where I wanted action, Michael wanted to explore possibilities. Where I sought structure, he sought connection. He liked to verbalize his thoughts aloud. I like to organize mine first.

Early on, I took his brainstorming for indecision. He thought my focus on detail meant I didn't value his ideas.

Taking the DISC together helped us name what was happening. He wasn't trying to avoid a decision. He was ideating. I wasn't dismissing his ideas. I was sorting them through my C-D lens.

We learned that when we hit friction, we pause. That understanding changed the temperature for our conversations. It brought softness where there could have been tension..

In marriage, just like in leadership, trust is built in the quiet acknowledgments. The subtle choice to listen differently. That choice—every time—is in the details.

Understanding someone's communication style is an act of compassion, not control.

I've learned that in marriage as in all human interaction we should:

- Pause before reacting.
- Clarify before assuming.
- Lean into strengths—especially under stress.

What About Other Personality Models?

DISC isn't the only model out there. Many people find insight through tools like the Enneagram, Myers-Briggs (MBTI), or StrengthsFinder. Each has its strengths and applications. I've chosen to focus on DISC in this chapter because of its direct connection to observable behavior, communication, and leadership dynamics. It's not about which model is best, it's about what works for you.

> ***Understanding people isn't about memorizing traits—***
> ***it's about noticing patterns, listening closely,***
> ***and learning to see beyond your own lens.***

Acknowledgment of Influence

I owe much of my DISC journey to Dr. Robert Rohm, who not only taught me the nuances of the model but also trained me to administer it with insight and integrity. Through his guidance, I've been able to use DISC not just as a leadership tool, but as a bridge to better relationships, clearer communication, and deeper understanding. I've trained my own team—and many others—on how DISC can be a powerful framework to strengthen work, life, and love. What began as a professional development exercise became a personal transformation.

Soul Pause

Your Personality in Practice

Prompt 1: What is your dominant DISC style? How does it help or hinder you in work or relationships?

Prompt 2: Think of someone whose behavior frustrates you. Could their DISC style be different from yours?

Prompt 3: What small shift could you make this week to better connect with someone close to you?

Communication Tips by Style

If they are ... Try this

High D | Be direct and brief. Focus on results.

High I | Be enthusiastic. Let them talk. Recognize their ideas.

High S | Be patient. Provide stability and clear timelines.

High C | Be precise. Offer details. Give time to process.

Final Reflection: The Beauty of Different Rhythms

Recognitions, quiet adaptations, and thoughtful responses.

All of it—every shift, every insight—begins by seeing people clearly.

And seeing people clearly? That's in the details.

Understanding people doesn't start with frameworks. It starts with focus—by noticing the hesitation before a response, the shift in tone. DISC gave me the language. But attention gave me the insight. That's where the transformation lives: in the details.

The Details Beneath

1. **Understanding Behavior Through DISC:** The DISC model helped me recognize that people's behavior often masks their intent. It taught me to pay attention to subtle cues—a pause, a change in tone—and to look beyond the action to the why. The framework gave me the language, but presence gave me the clarity.

2. **Bridging Differences in Marriage:** DISC helped illuminate how my husband and I processed information differently. Understanding our distinct styles allowed us to extend more grace, adjust our expectations, and strengthen our communication.

3. **Preventing Conflict Through Anticipation:** In leadership, DISC became a preventative tool. By knowing how different personalities respond to pressure, I could anticipate needs and reduce friction before it started.

4. **Listening for Strengths:** Paying attention to how others express themselves helped me uncover their natural

strengths. DISC shifted my listening from evaluation to appreciation, from correction to connection.

5. **DISC as a Blueprint, Not a Box:** Labels can limit—but DISC, when used well, liberates. It offers a blueprint for deeper understanding, not a cage. When paired with genuine attention, it becomes a map to more empathetic, effective relationships.

*Further reading and selected references for this chapter are available in the Notes & Sources section at the end of this book.

Small Moments Write the Story of Our Lives

The Whisper, Not the Wind

"We expect God to shout. But often, He whispers.
And the whisper is enough."
— Dr. Danita Johnson Woods

We are conditioned to search for God in the big, the bold, and the breathtaking. We look for signs in the storms, confirmation in the thunder, and guidance wrapped in flashing lights. But often, God does not come through the earthquake or the fire. He meets us in the stillness—in the breath between questions, in the quiet tug on the heart, in the peace that passes understanding.

Faith isn't just built through miracles. It's shaped in the silence.

It's not always the answered prayer that strengthens us—but the quiet waiting that teaches us how to hear.

In this chapter, we journey with Jada, whose life turned not because of a dramatic revelation, but because of a whisper she finally trusted. Her story—and Elijah's ancient one—reminds us that God's guidance doesn't always come wrapped in spectacle. Sometimes it comes wrapped in quiet assurance.

This is a chapter about the sacredness of silence.

About how peace can be the answer.

And about how the whisper can be more powerful than the wind.

CHAPTER FOURTEEN

The Whisper, Not the Wind

"The miracle isn't always in the moment. Sometimes, it's in the quiet courage to trust it."
— Dr. Danita Johnson Woods

The Story: Jada's Whisper

Jada had always believed in the power of prayer. She was the type of woman who carried Scripture in her wallet, who left voice notes of encouragement for friends, and who started each morning with coffee and quiet time. Her life wasn't perfect, but it was anchored.

At least, it used to be.

In the months leading up to her decision, things had shifted. The nonprofit organization she helped build from the ground up was changing. Leadership had become toxic. The mission felt lost. Every Monday felt heavier than the last, and each morning, her commute felt like she was driving away from peace. She had stayed longer than she should have—out of loyalty, fear, and the quiet guilt that maybe she was the problem.

Sometimes the soul knows long before the mind catches up.

Jada had reached a crossroads. She could leave and risk uncertainty … or stay and risk her spirit.

She journaled. She fasted. She sought advice from mentors, attended a women's conference, and even got away for a weekend retreat. And while all the noise around her pointed to change, her soul felt stuck in neutral. She kept asking, "God, where are You in this? Just tell me what to do."

She expected clarity to hit like a lightning bolt.

It didn't.

Then came a Tuesday morning. Nothing remarkable about it—gray skies, laundry half-folded, emails piling up. She sat at the kitchen table, Bible open, coffee cooling, mind racing. Her prayers felt hollow, more like pleading than communion.

Sometimes the soul knows long before the mind catches up.

And then—something small.

A phrase surfaced. Trust me, even now.

It wasn't loud. It wasn't new. But it felt settled—like it didn't come from her.

She paused. Listened again.

Nothing more came. No confirmation email from heaven. No miraculous sign. Just a subtle shift—a loosening of fear. A breath of peace she hadn't felt in months.

"Peace is often the answer—when words never come."

The clarity didn't come with bullet points. Just one thing: leave.

Not because she had another job. Not because she had it all figured out.

But because she finally believed she wouldn't fall.

Later, when a friend asked what had changed, Jada smiled. "It wasn't one big thing. Just a whisper I didn't ignore."

That was how she knew it was God.

Sometimes God moves in silence so we learn how to listen.

The Sound of Stillness: Elijah's Story

Jada's moment mirrors the ancient story of Elijah in 1 Kings 19. Fresh off a spiritual high—calling down fire from heaven and proving God's power in a dramatic showdown with false prophets—Elijah should've felt invincible. Instead, he found himself running for his life.

Queen Jezebel, furious about the public defeat of her prophets, sent a death threat Elijah's way: "By this time tomorrow, you'll be as dead as they are."

And just like that, fear overwhelmed faith.

God doesn't always come in power.
Sometimes He comes in peace.

Elijah fled into the wilderness, collapsing under a broom tree and telling God he'd had enough. "Take my life," he said. "I'm no better than those who came before me." He was depleted—physically, emotionally, spiritually. He wasn't just scared; he was done.

And yet, God didn't rebuke him. He didn't ask for more. He let Elijah rest. He sent an angel to feed him. Twice. Then He led Elijah on a 40-day journey to Horeb—the mountain of God.

There, Elijah hid in a cave. He had done everything right. He had been faithful, passionate, and obedient. But even with all that, he didn't know what to do next.

And so, he waited for God to speak.

There came a wind—strong enough to shatter rocks. But God was not in the wind. Then an earthquake shook the ground. But God was not in the earthquake. Next came fire. But God was not in the fire.

Then—a still, small voice.

It wasn't just about how God spoke. It was about what Elijah had to do in order to hear. He had to slow down. He had to empty himself of fear, noise, and exhaustion to be filled with something deeper than adrenaline. The voice didn't shake the mountain—but it shook him back into purpose.

The whisper didn't change the world—but it changed Elijah.

God reminded him that he wasn't alone, that there was still work to do, and that he didn't have to carry the mission by himself. It was in the stillness—not the spectacle—that Elijah found his footing again.

Adapted from 1 Kings 19, paraphrased and interpreted for reflection.

Tuning Into the Whisper

Like Jada, many of us wait for clarity wrapped in lightning bolts. But God's voice often shows up in far more subtle ways:

- A scripture that won't leave your spirit.
- A line from a song that echoes at just the right moment.
- A dream you can't shake.
- An unexpected sense of peace when everything should be chaotic.
- A "no" that doesn't come with explanation—but is still clearly no.

These are not random. These are divine details.

Spiritual maturity is learning to recognize that presence doesn't always come with volume. Sometimes God withdraws the fire and wind—not to abandon us—but to teach us that His voice doesn't need to compete with chaos. It simply needs space.

Divine Timing Is a Detail

Jada didn't get her answer all at once. She got peace. She got clarity in increments.

And maybe that's the deeper truth: sometimes God withholds the full picture because He's drawing us into a slower, more faithful rhythm.

> ***Spiritual maturity isn't waiting for thunder—***
> ***it's recognizing the hush.***

What if the silence is part of the strategy?

What if the pause is part of the preparation?

God often answers slowly—because He's shaping you while you wait.

Soul Pause: Listening for the Whisper

Take a moment to breathe.

Are you looking for God in the noise? In the hustle?
In the demands?

What if He's already speaking—in the whisper? In the rest?
In the silence?

Where in your life might you need to slow down... so you can actually hear?

In a world full of noise, God often waits for stillness. This week, create a sacred space to hear what your spirit already knows.

Today, try this:

- Sit in silence for five minutes—no phone, no agenda.
- Reflect on what keeps rising in your heart when everything else quiets down.
- Ask: What has God been whispering that I've been too busy to hear?

Journal Moment:

When was the last time peace—not certainty—guided your next step?

What areas of your life feel loud right now? Where can you lean into stillness instead of striving?

Whispers don't demand your attention. They wait for your surrender.

How God Speaks in the Details

Sometimes it's not about a "word from the Lord"—it's about a shift in your spirit.

Here are a few small, sacred signs that often carry deep spiritual direction:

- A pause that feels holy

That moment you feel led to wait—just a little longer.

- A yes with no striving

You're not forcing the door open. You're walking through it with peace.

- A no that comes gently, but firmly

A check in your spirit, a delayed opportunity, a redirection that won't leave you.

- Divine repetition

When the same scripture, lyric, or phrase keeps showing up, pay attention. That's not coincidence—it's confirmation.

Tiny Truth: God rarely shouts over your chaos. He waits for your consent to quiet it.

Final Reflection: A Faith That Listens

We live in a world that rewards volume. But the life of faith asks something quieter: discernment.

The God who parted seas also whispered in a cave. The same Jesus who raised Lazarus also slipped away to pray alone. Power doesn't always look loud. Sometimes, it looks like a breath before the decision. A held silence before the answer. A question asked in prayer and met, not with a booming response, but with a slow unfolding of clarity.

You don't need a dramatic sign to know you're being led. You just need to be still enough to trust the whisper.

The Details Beneath

1. "Trust me, even now" — Echoes the quiet confidence often described in contemplative prayer traditions. Similar language appears in Warren's reflections on divine presence amid grief and waiting (Warren, 2021).

2. Jada's emotional fatigue reflects what theologians call the "dark night of the soul," a concept explored deeply in Warren (2021) and classically rooted in spiritual literature. It speaks to times when faith feels dry but remains formative.

3. The narrative of Elijah in 1 Kings 19:11 12, where God reveals Himself not through fire or wind, but a still, small voice, is one of the clearest scriptural examples of divine subtlety.

4. The phrase "peace that passes understanding" comes from Philippians 4:7 and is often cited in modern spiritual guides like Kong (2021) and Myers (2022) as a marker of divine affirmation.

5. Divine repetition—when phrases, scriptures, or lyrics appear multiple times—may be interpreted as a spiritual nudge or confirmation. Virkler (2020) explores this as a key feature of discerning God's voice.

6. The idea that God doesn't compete with chaos but waits for stillness is grounded in contemplative Christian traditions and supported by insights from Hagin's (2014) revised work, which emphasizes internal peace as a filter for guidance.

7. The slow unfolding of clarity—rather than instant answers—is a theme echoed in Blackaby (2023), who stresses that divine timing often shapes character before it offers direction.

*Further reading and selected references for this chapter are available in the Notes & Sources section at the end of this book.

Small Moments Write the Story of Our Lives

The Mustard Seed Effect—How Small Observations Advance Science

"In every scientific breakthrough, there's a quiet spark—
a single detail brave enough to be noticed."
— Dr. Danita Johnson Woods

Breakthroughs in science don't always come through explosions of genius. Sometimes, they arrive through a pause. A question. A small, almost-dismissed observation that lingers just long enough to be explored.

This chapter is about one such moment. A patient. A physician. A quiet act of curiosity that defied conventional thinking and opened the door to a lifelong transformation in how healing is understood.

What follows is more than a medical story. It is a reminder that in both science and life, it is often the smallest voices, the most ordinary details, that carry the greatest power to shift everything.

Because sometimes, the seed of innovation isn't bold.

It's barely visible—until it grows.

CHAPTER FIFTEEN

The Mustard Seed Effect—How Small Observations Advance Science

"Breakthroughs aren't accidents—they're the reward for noticing what others overlook."
— Dr. Danita Johnson Woods

Rather than summarizing, I've asked Dr. Chiedu Nchekwube to share this moment in his own words. What follows is his firsthand account of a patient, a pause, and a paradigm shift.

A Small Event Like the Mustard Seed, with a Great Footprint, and Life-Long Professional Impact

Practicing allopathic or conventional medicine for many years—as I was trained to do—the last treatment I would have considered for managing uncontrolled hypertension was aged garlic. Yet learning to use garlic as a treatment transformed my entire approach to medicine. It marked a shift from strictly Allopathic or Conventional Medicine to a career in Integrative and Functional Medicine that has spanned over 35 years.

In every scientific breakthrough, there's a whisper—a detail that dared to be heard.

This transformation began in the 1980s, when exploring alternative treatments was considered risky for a physician. Such a transition often spelled the end of a conventional medical practice. Still, everything changed because of a single patient.

She was a middle-aged woman, interested in empowering herself to manage her health with minimal pharmaceutical intervention—a rarity in that era. Despite her commitment to lifestyle changes, including diet and exercise, her hypertension remained uncontrolled. I eventually prescribed Captopril, a drug commonly used at the time, especially for patients with hypertension and congestive heart failure.

As we monitored her treatment, I adjusted the Captopril dosage as needed, seeing some improvement, though inconsistently. Then something unexpected happened. Her blood pressure became consistently stable, yet her prescription bottle appeared untouched. Upon questioning her, she revealed she had stopped taking the Captopril months earlier.

Instead, she had begun eating garlic cloves and drinking garlic water daily. She explained that folk medicine had long used garlic to manage high blood pressure. At first, I was skeptical. But her stable readings and commitment inspired me to research garlic's medicinal properties. What I found humbled me.

Innovation isn't always a new invention—it's often rediscovered wisdom."

Garlic, a humble bulb, has been extensively researched for its cardiovascular benefits. Studies show it can reduce systolic blood pressure by 10–12 mm Hg in hypertensive patients, comparable to some medications. Aged garlic extract has also been shown to slow coronary plaque progression and stabilize vulnerable arterial plaques. These effects are attributed to bioactive sulfur compounds, especially S-allyl cysteine, which provide anti-inflammatory, antioxidant, and vasodilatory benefits.

This revelation opened the door to a much broader body of evidence supporting natural interventions—nutrition, movement, meditation, and prayer—that had not been part of my conventional training. I began to pursue Integrative Medicine, a holistic model that considers the physical, spiritual, emotional, and lifestyle factors affecting health.

In this model, care becomes personalized and collaborative. The patient takes the wheel, while the physician serves as a navigator toward the safe harbor of well-being and a long health span. This approach rekindled my love for medicine, prevented burnout, and expanded my ability to serve patients through leadership and advocacy in Integrative Medicine.

"Innovation isn't always a new invention—
it's often rediscovered wisdom."

That single moment—a patient's choice to use garlic—was like a mustard seed. It grew into a paradigm shift, influencing my patients, students, and colleagues for decades. It reminds me daily that no detail is too small to change everything.

What seemed like a folk remedy became the gateway to a revolution in care.

Microlesson: Listening Like a Scientist

What if the real breakthroughs aren't hiding in laboratories, but in listening rooms? What if science moves forward not only with research—but with respect for lived experience? That's the detail that struck me. Not the garlic—but the willingness to be curious about it.

In my own work, I've seen similar shifts. A staff member's question that sparked a department-wide change. A forgotten line in a grant that unlocked new funding. The detail isn't always garlic—but the principle is the same.

Transformation begins in stillness.

What struck me most about Dr. Nchekwube's experience wasn't just the garlic—it was the humility to listen. In healthcare, leadership, and life, how often do we override the quiet wisdom around us because it doesn't come packaged in credentials or protocol? I've learned that transformation rarely announces itself. It takes root quietly, like a seed beneath the soil.

Have you ever dismissed a detail—something small someone said or did—that later turned out to be meaningful? What would it look like to approach each moment as potentially life-shaping?

Write about a time you were surprised by the impact of a small event or choice. What shifted in you or around you?

Seeds of Discovery

1. Take a movement to think about the "garlic moments" in your own life—The small overlooked details that turned out to hold unexpected power. Perhaps it was and offhand comment, a simple home remedy, or a quiet inner nudge that let you toward a better path. Science may call it observation. Faith may call it revelation. Whatever the name, it is worth honoring. What small truth is waiting for you to notice it today?

2. The mustard seed reminds us that God often hides the greatest power in the smallest places. A whisper in your spirit, a gentle nudge toward a new idea, a humble ingredient like garlic—these can become the very instruments of transformation. Ask yourself: What tiny seed has God placed in my path that I have yet to plant?

Garlic and the Science of Details

- Garlic supplements can reduce systolic blood pressure by 10–12 mm Hg.
- S-allyl cysteine provides antioxidant, anti-inflammatory, and vasodilatory effects.
- Garlic has shown promise in stabilizing arterial plaques and supporting cardiovascular health.
- Integrative Medicine incorporates nutrition, natural therapies, and conventional treatments for holistic care. A single patient's story transformed decades of clinical practice."

Final Reflection: Where Transformation Takes Root

A single patient's courage to question conventional wisdom sparked a ripple that would change how a physician viewed the practice of medicine. Garlic—a humble kitchen ingredient—became a door to a broader, more integrated, more human view of health.

This story reminds us that innovation doesn't always require invention. Sometimes, it requires attention—to the details, to the murmurs, and to the wisdom that may be hiding in plain sight.

Small choices, when listened to, can echo through an entire profession.

Precision isn't just about data—it's about attention.

Trust the nudge to investigate, even if the idea sounds simple.

Track what others ignore.

Don't dismiss what's unfamiliar—ask why it works.

The Details Beneath

1. The patient's success with garlic led Dr. Nchekwube to reconsider conventional approaches and study alternative therapies.
2. Garlic has been used for centuries in traditional medicine for its health benefits, especially related to cardiovascular health, immune support and antimicrobial properties.
3. The concept of Integrative Medicine combines conventional and evidence-based natural therapies to treat the whole person, emphasizing patient-centered care.
4. Dr. Nchekwube's transformation reflects how one small moment in a clinical setting can spark systemic change in practice.

*Further reading and selected references for this chapter are available in the Notes & Sources section at the end of this book.

The Algorithim and Me: Javiar's Aha Moment

"The smallest click can steer the largest consequences—but awareness can reclaim the wheel."
— Dr. Danita Johnson Woods

We live in a time when what we see, what we believe, and even what we feel can be influenced by forces we barely notice.

An algorithm doesn't shout. It doesn't demand.

It hums—subtly, persistently, shaping our realities one scroll, one like, one suggested video at a time.

It's easy to assume we are making conscious choices online. But too often, the choices are made for us—curated, filtered, and fed back to us in narrower and narrower streams of thought. Over time, those digital details—what we click, what we watch, what we share—start weaving invisible threads through our thinking, our relationships, and even our sense of self.

This chapter is about recognizing those threads. About realizing that freedom isn't just about the ability to choose—it's about noticing when the power to choose is quietly slipping away.

Through Javier's story, we see how small, unnoticed shifts in his digital life shaped much bigger shifts in his real life. And how reclaiming awareness, one decision at a time, helped him take back not just his feed—but his future.

Because in a world increasingly designed to guide our choices without our permission, the most powerful thing we can do is to wake up to the details—and choose for ourselves.

The digital world may shape our feed, but we shape our future.

CHAPTER SIXTEEN

The Algorithim and Me: Javiar's Aha Moment

"Breakthroughs aren't accidents—they're the reward for noticing what others overlook."
— Dr. Danita Johnson Woods

The Narrowing Feed

This is my story. I'm Javier Cardona—Black, Puerto Rican, and stubborn from birth—raised by a single mom who didn't play about politics. When I was 15, I thought I knew everything. I believed my social media feed reflected my own voice, my own beliefs. But it was already shaping me in ways I couldn't yet see.

My mom tried to keep me grounded. She watched the debates, read the news, and made sure I understood what was going on in the world—even when I didn't want to. She would sit me down and explain why voting mattered, why history mattered, why people fought and died for rights we still don't always get.

Be aware of how the algorithm shapes our beliefs and take control of our narratives.

At 15, though, I was more drawn to the loud voices online. It started innocently enough: a few viral debate clips—Ben Shapiro "destroying" college students, and other right-wing content railing against "wokeness" and "cancel culture."

The algorithm fed me more: conspiracies about vaccines, feminism, and free speech under attack.

At first, it felt like I had found clarity, like I was seeing the truth no one else dared to say out loud.

We have to be aware of how the algorithm shapes our beliefs and take control of our narratives.

It was subtle at first.

News outlets I once trusted began to feel like echo chambers. Ads seemed to know my fears before I could even name them.

I wasn't just finding information anymore—it was finding me. And it was shaping me.

The Wake-Up Call

I remember a local election season where the stakes were high.

Scrolling through my phone, everything I saw supported one narrative. It made the other side seem villainous, incompetent, or worse.

It became easy to believe what I was being fed, even when it conflicted with my own lived experiences—and with the values my mom had worked so hard to instill.

That's when I realized: "I couldn't just vote for vibes; I had to vote for reality."

In 2024, I voted for the president for the first time. It was a hard choice. I didn't agree with everything on either side. But when I stood in that voting booth, I thought about my mom, my community, and the future I wanted to help build.

I couldn't afford to be a passive participant anymore.

Choosing a Different Path

"It was a wake-up call—I could either continue down this path or forge my own."

Freedom isn't wrestled from the world around you. It's reclaimed in the small choices you make within.

Taking control of my narrative meant more than changing what I clicked.

It meant reclaiming my critical thinking.

It meant stepping away from spaces that mocked single moms, dismissed Latino culture, and acted like racism was just made up.

It meant listening to the growing unease inside me—the part that asked, "Are they talking about me too?"

I began expanding my feed.

During my sophomore and junior years, I followed creators who looked like me.

I read more from people outside the U.S., listened to podcasts that weren't just yelling at their audiences, and started questioning the easy answers I'd once clung to. In that journey, I stopped being a passive consumer.

In that moment, I realized I wasn't just a passive consumer of information; I was an active participant in shaping my community.

And that realization changed everything.

The Ripple Effect

I thought about all the moments I had argued with friends, or distanced myself from family—especially my mom—over headlines I never even fact-checked.

How many relationships have quietly eroded because we are living in different digital realities?

The algorithm hadn't just influenced what I thought. It had shaped what—and who—I trusted.

It also took a toll on my mental health. Being in spaces where people joked about "the Jewish question" or belittled people of color left scars.

For a long time, I felt excluded—even from the spaces I had defended. I began to wonder: If something as small as a click could create distance between people, could a conscious choice begin to heal it?

The smallest click can steer the largest consequences—
but awareness can reclaim the wheel.

Our digital lives are not isolated from our real ones. They ripple into dinner conversations, family gatherings, local elections, and personal dreams. The smallest online habits can lead to the largest offline consequences. Choosing differently online is an act of love offline—love for ourselves, our communities, and our collective future.

Freedom isn't wrestled from the world around you. It's reclaimed in the small choices you make within.

Reclaiming Your Digital Narrative

1. Think about the last time you were influenced by something you saw online without realizing it at first.

2. What beliefs, emotions, or actions did it nudge you toward?

3. Now reflect: How can you be more intentional in curating what you consume?

4. What voices or perspectives have you not heard lately—and how can you seek them out?

Your feed is your choice. Curate wisely.

Protecting Your Mind in a Digital Age

- Diversify your sources. Follow people, outlets, and thinkers outside of your usual views.
- Pause before reacting. Not everything urgent deserves your immediate emotional investment.
- Use technology mindfully. Algorithms are powerful—but your awareness is more powerful.
- Unfollow manipulation. If a page, brand, or person consistently stirs fear or outrage, reconsider your engagement
- Remember: You are not the product. Your time, attention, and beliefs are valuable. Protect them.

Javier's Reflection

Now I'm older.
I still question everything.
I still get skeptical.
But I also try to stay grounded, informed, and open.
The algorithm doesn't influence me anymore.

I choose what I see. I check sources. I talk with people who challenge me.

I live with my eyes open.

Final Reflection: Taking Back the Small Choices That Shape Everything

In a world that runs on speed, noise, and algorithms, real freedom is found in stillness, awareness, and small acts of intention.

The clicks we make. The articles we share. The voices we amplify or ignore. They may feel insignificant in the moment, but over time, they sculpt the reality we live in.

Javier's story reminds us: it's not just about guarding what we believe. It's about tending how we believe—who we listen to, what we question, and how we hold space for truth even when it's quieter than outrage.

You don't have to be an expert to protect your mind.

You don't have to be perfect to reclaim your power.

You just have to wake up to the small, sacred choices you're making every day.

Because in the end, it's not the loudest feed or the flashiest post that defines you.

It's the quiet decision to think for yourself.

To listen deeper.

To choose better.

It's in the details—and the details are where freedom begins.

In a world driven by fast clicks and curated feeds, remembering the power of small, intentional choices is how we reclaim our lives—detail by detail.

The Details Beneath

1. The impact of algorithms on belief systems and political polarization has been well-documented, including in The Social Dilemma and Pew Research data on digital news habits.

2. Viral content and the role of online influencers—such as Ben Shapiro—have been studied for their impact on adolescent political formation.

3. Terms like "digital echo chambers" and algorithmic bias are explored in the work of scholars such as Safiya Noble and Zeynep Tufekci.

4. The phrase "you are not the product" reflects critiques of surveillance capitalism, particularly as discussed by Shoshana Zuboff.

5. Mental health concerns related to online radicalization and hate exposure have been raised by public health researchers and organizations like the Center for Humane Technology.

6. The quote "Freedom isn't wrestled from the world around you. It's reclaimed in the small choices you make within" is original to this book.

*Further reading and selected references for this chapter are available in the Notes & Sources section at the end of this book.

Modern Echoes—How Small Digital Acts Fuel Movements Today

"Social media is the new pulpit, and one post can become a movement."
— Dr. Danita Johnson Woods

Change doesn't always roar into history. Sometimes, it taps quietly against a screen. In a digital world fueled by scrolling and swiping, we often underestimate the gravity of a single act: a video recorded, a truth shared, a voice raised online.

But make no mistake—small digital choices have built movements, reshaped narratives, and cracked open systems once thought unshakable.

Today, activism can start with a post.

Awareness can start with a click.

Courage can start with a trembling hand hitting "record."

This chapter is a tribute to the people who understood that power isn't always about having a platform. It's about using whatever you have to bear witness.

Because even the smallest digital echo can awaken something ancient, something sacred: the collective fight for truth.

CHAPTER SEVENTEEN

Modern Echoes—How Small Digital Acts Fuel Movements Today

The echo of truth, even when whispered online, can stir a generation.
— Dr. Danita Johnson Woods

One Post, One Voice, One Spark: The Courage of a Seventeen-Year-Old Girl

A teenage girl named Darnella Frazier stood on the corner of 38th Street and Chicago Avenue in Minneapolis. The day was May 25, 2020. She wasn't a journalist. She wasn't an activist. She was simply walking her younger cousin to the store when she witnessed a moment that would mark a generation—a Black man, George Floyd, pinned to the ground beneath the knee of a white police officer.

Instead, with trembling hands and a sense that something wasn't right, she pulled out her phone and pressed record. In those nine minutes and twenty-nine seconds, the world witnessed the slow, brutal death of George Floyd. Her video, raw and shaky, carried a clarity that no bodycam footage, police statement, or edited news clip ever could. It was the truth, unfiltered and undeniable.

Social media is the new pulpit, and one post can become a movement.

She didn't shout or protest at the moment. She simply recorded. And that small act—one post, one voice—ignited a spark that would burn across the globe.

> *"I opened my phone and went to my camera, because I knew that if I didn't, no one would believe me."*
> — Darnella Frazier (during Derek Chauvin's trial as reported by *The Guardian*.)

That decision—small in action, massive in consequence—became one of the most critical pieces of evidence in the fight for justice in modern history. Her short video, taken through tears and trembling, was not just documentation. It was disruption, defiance, and digital courage in its purest form.

Digital Witness as Moral Witness

In another era, George Floyd's death might have been explained away. Internal reports. Conflicting testimonies. Lack of visual proof. But in the age of smartphones and social media, Darnella became the world's witness. Her video stripped away plausible deniability and forced people to look, listen, and feel the weight of what they were seeing.

There was no music. No filter. No angle to make it easier to swallow.

That's the power of a post rooted in truth.

Darnella's video wasn't just a post. It became evidence. It became a mirror. It became a movement.

Within hours, the footage had spread across platforms—Facebook, Twitter, Instagram, WhatsApp—each share a digital echo calling for justice. People poured into the streets. Murals went up. Statues came down. Corporations released carefully worded statements. Police departments re-examined their training, and some were forced to confront what they'd long denied: that systemic racism was not just past tense—it was breathing, violent, and present.

World leaders commented. Activists organized. Children asked hard questions. And in the center of it all was the courage of a 17-year-old girl who simply refused to be silent.

The Ripple of a Single Act

Darnella's simple act of recording catalyzed the largest civil rights movement since the 1960s. Billions of voices would rise. Over 60 countries would march. Murals would rise. Streets would be renamed. Conversations about policing, race, and equity would flood boardrooms, classrooms, and living rooms alike. And yet, Darnella never saw herself as a hero.

"When I look at George Floyd, I look at my dad, I look at my brothers, I look at my cousins, my uncles. It could have been them."
— Darnella Frazier, during Derek Chauvin's trial

In that moment, her instinct wasn't political. It was personal. But personal becomes political when pain is public—when the truth refuses to be buried; when the phone is lifted and injustice is caught in mid-breath.

When the Small Act Is the Spark

Darnella didn't need a megaphone, a platform, or a brand. She needed clarity. A conviction to bear witness. A willingness to press record. In a world obsessed with likes and followers, her story reminds us: Truth needs neither. It only needs courage.

Darnella didn't know her video would fuel one of the largest civil rights uprisings in modern history. She didn't set out to be a hero.

She was scared. She was traumatized. She said later that she wished she could have done more.

But what she did do—bravely, instinctively—was enough to change the world.

Because sometimes, the revolution doesn't start with a megaphone. Sometimes it starts with a phone in the hands of a girl who knows that silence is too high a price to pay.

Darnella's video reminds us that justice is often born in the quiet decisions no one sees coming: to stand still, to bear witness, to press record. She didn't need a podium to change the world—just a phone and the will to speak without saying a word.

Personal becomes political when pain is public.

"Even though this was a traumatic life-changing experience for me, I'm proud of myself. If it weren't for my video, the world wouldn't have known the truth. I own that."

—as reported by NPR

Other Young Voices Who Sparked Change

Darnella's courage is part of a global movement powered by young people with vision, conviction, and smartphones. These modern truth-tellers have disrupted injustice in quiet, simple ways that ripple across the world.

- **Emma González,** survivor of the 2018 Parkland school shooting, used her voice and digital presence to ignite a youth-led gun reform movement. stood before millions and said "We call BS." Her impassioned speech, filmed and shared across platforms, became a rallying cry for gun reform, giving rise to the March for Our Lives movement.

- **Amariyanna "Mari" Copeny,** Amariyanna "Mari" Copeny—known as "Little Miss Flint"—was just 8 years old when a single tweet to then-President Obama brought national attention to the Flint water crisis, prompting his visit and resulting in millions in relief funding.
- **Greta Thunberg,** whose solitary climate strike shared online sparked a global movement of environmental youth activism. A teenager who started a strike outside the Swedish Parliament and used Instagram and Twitter to document her protest. Her single act of refusal became a global youth movement, with millions joining in weekly climate marches.

What ties all of these voices together isn't fame or funding. It's clarity. It's the unwavering belief that a small digital act—one video, one tweet, one post—can shake the system. And they're right.

These young people didn't wait for the world to change. They posted. They marched. They recorded. And they shook systems.

What connects them is not influence—it's intentionality. They understood something we often forget:

Small things done with great clarity can change everything.

The Thread That Connects: Details Matter

This is what *It's in the Details* is about. The world often looks to big titles, grand gestures, or sweeping legislation to define change. But real transformation? It often begins in the unnoticed corners—in the quiet decision to not look away. In the impulse to document injustice. In the refusal to let a story be buried.

Darnella didn't intend to change the world. She simply told the truth.

But that's the secret.

Telling the truth is never a small thing!

Scripture Reflection:

"And you will know the truth, and the truth will set you free."

— John 8:32 (NIV)

This is not just a Bible verse—it's a liberation strategy.

Truth is not just something to know. It is something to live, share, and honor—especially in a world that depends on distraction and denial.

In every generation, there is someone who stands up—or stands still—with trembling hands and a steady soul, and says, "This is what happened." Their voice may crack. Their hands may shake. But they speak, record, post, share… and the walls begin to tremble.

Because the truth, when shared, makes room for freedom—not just for the one who tells it, but for us all.

Ancestral Echoes: The Sacred Power of Bearing Witness

What Darnella Frazier did wasn't new.

It was ancient.

From the hush harbors where enslaved Africans whispered truth to one another in secret, to the coded verses of Negro spirituals that masked escape plans as praise, to the kitchen-table testimonies of the Civil Rights Movement—Black people have always understood that truth-telling is a spiritual act. A form of resistance. A form of healing.

Truth is not just something to know. It is something to live, share, and honor.

In a world built on denying our pain, our power has always come from our willingness to name it.

Darnella, standing on that street corner, joined a long lineage of Black women who said, "No more silence." She became the griot of her generation—capturing and sharing the raw, unvarnished truth in a way that shook the world awake.

We see this echoed in the lives of women like:

- **Ida B. Wells,** who risked her life to document lynchings, knowing that truth could be fatal—but silence was worse.
- **Fannie Lou Hamer,** who told her story of forced sterilization and voter suppression before national cameras, saying plainly: "I'm sick and tired of being sick and tired."
- And now, **Darnella,** whose smartphone became her pulpit.

These women didn't wait for permission. They understood that testimony is sacred, and bearing witness is an offering—not just to justice, but to God.

Modern Call to Action: Your Platform Is Your Pulpit

You may not have a million followers. You may not think of yourself as an activist.

But you have a voice. A platform. A story. And the courage to not look away.

Your Instagram story? That's a testimony.

Your TikTok? A modern psalm.

Your repost, your caption, your comment? Those are digital seeds. And seeds grow movements.

Testimony is sacred. Bearing witness is an offering—not just to justice, but to God.

You don't have to go viral to be valuable. You just have to be intentional.

Because it's *in the details.*

The decision to speak up when someone makes an inappropriate joke.

The courage to share your own story of injustice or survival.

The integrity to post something meaningful when it would be easier to stay quiet and polished and liked.

We were never meant to be spectators, not in life, and certainly not online.

The Sacred Scroll: Your Feed as a Living Record

What if we stopped viewing our feeds as highlight reels—and started treating them like sacred scrolls?

A living, breathing collection of what we care about.

Who we stand with.

What we're willing to name.

What we believe is worth remembering.

You don't have to post everything. But what you do choose to share, support, or say—let it count.

Even the smallest echo can awaken something ancient.

You are not "just" a user.

You are not "just" scrolling.

You are shaping the world—one detail, one decision, one digital act at a time.

So, take your place.

Lift your voice.

And let the echoes begin.

Soul Pause

Small Acts, Wide Ripples

Think of a time when you used your voice—online or off—to stand up for someone else, or when someone stood up for you. What happened? What changed? What part of you still remembers?

1. When have I seen something wrong and chosen silence? What held me back?"
2. "If I could shine a light on injustice with one small act, what would it be?"
3. "Am I using my platform—no matter how small—to make truth visible?"
4. "What is mine to witness, even when it's uncomfortable?"
5. "How do I honor the power of my own voice—even when I feel small?"

The Courage to Record

Not every act of influence begins with intention.

Sometimes it begins with instinct.

A young girl stands on a sidewalk.
A moment unfolds that no one planned to document.
History does not announce itself before it happens.

It simply asks:

Will someone see?
Will someone stay?
Will someone refuse to turn away?

In that moment, witnessing becomes responsibility.

The act of holding a camera steady is not passive.
It is a decision to remain present
when fear suggests retreat.

Digital tools can distract.
But they can also preserve truth
when memory might otherwise be denied.

What was captured did not create injustice—
it revealed it.

And in revealing, it shifted what the world could no longer ignore.

Sometimes change begins not with a march,
or a speech,
or a plan—

but with someone choosing
not to look away.

Final Reflection: The Echo of a Single Voice

In a world that moves fast and forgets easily, may we be found faithful—to truth, to justice, and to the quiet courage of bearing witness.

Reflection Prayer

For the Strength to Witness

When truth unfolds in front of me,
give me the courage to remain present.
When fear urges distance,
steady my resolve.
Help me understand that seeing
is not always comfortable,
and presence is not always easy.
Grant me the strength
to hold space for what is real,
even when it disrupts what is familiar.
Let me not shrink from moments
that ask for quiet bravery.
Teach me that influence is not always loud—
sometimes it is simply the refusal
to turn away.
May I honor the responsibility
that comes with awareness.
And when history passes near me,
let me be someone
who does not look away.

— Dr. Danita Johnson Woods

The Details Beneath

1. Darnella Frazier's decision to record George Floyd's murder and testify in court was pivotal. Her courage was acknow-l edged with a Pulitzer Prize special citation.

2. In interviews, Frazier expressed both the emotional toll and the pride she felt in taking action—highlighting the personal cost of digital activism.

3. Emma González's "We Call BS" speech became a viral rallying cry after the Parkland shooting, demonstrating the immediacy of youth-led digital movements.
4. In 2016, Mari Copeny (known as "Little Miss Flint") tweeted President Obama, drawing national attention to the Flint water crisis and prompting a federal response.

5. Greta Thunberg's solo climate strike in Sweden gained momentum through social media, sparking the international Fridays for Future movement.

6. "And you will know the truth, and the truth will set you free." — John 8:32 (NIV).

7. Ida B. Wells' groundbreaking investigative journalism exposed lynching in the U.S. and continues to shape public discourse on racial justice.

8. Fannie Lou Hamer's unforgettable quote—"I'm sick and tired of being sick and tired"—captured the exhaustion and resolve at the heart of the Civil Rights Movement.

*Further reading and selected references for this chapter are available in the Notes & Sources section at the end of this book.

Small Moments Write the Story of Our Lives

The Quiet Redline: Housing Discrimination

"Injustice doesn't always arrive with noise. Sometimes, it hides in silence—tucked inside policies, disguised as neutral maps, and reinforced by decisions no one questions anymore."
— Dr. Danita Johnson Woods

Not all injustice wears a uniform or carries a sign. Some slip quietly through the back door—approved by city councils, signed off in zoning meetings, and layered into neighborhood maps that look neutral on the surface but are anything but.

This chapter isn't just about redlining. It's about what happens when something unfair becomes normal. When the lines dividing us stop looking like lines—just streets, districts, boundaries. Harmless. Until you trace who gets what.

Redlining didn't come with protests or press releases. It came with pens and stamps. With phrases like "not ideal for lending." And though the laws have changed, the outcomes haven't. You can still see its fingerprints—in the schools our kids attend, the grocery stores we don't have, the property values that lag decades behind. This is the kind of injustice that runs silent but deep. But make no mistake: it speaks volumes. And if injustice can arrive quietly, then justice must speak clearly—and redraw what should never have been drawn at all.

CHAPTER EIGHTEEN

The Quiet Redline: Housing Discrimination

"The most dangerous lines are the ones we stop seeing — the ones drawn in silence, enforced by habit, and overlooked by history."
— Dr. Danita Johnson Woods

History often feels like a grand parade of decisions and declarations, led by people in power waving flags of certainty. But dig deeper, and you'll find a quieter story—the kind whispered behind closed doors or buried under the dust of forgotten files. Sometimes, it's not the speech that changed the world, but the one that was never given. Not the law that passed, but the one that lingered in draft form, unsigned and unspoken.

In a world shaped by actions, the details that go undone—missed telegrams, overlooked clauses, letters that never reached their destination—have tipped the scales of justice, delayed peace, and rewritten the fate of nations. This chapter is a meditation on what could have been—and what was—because someone missed the detail.

"Sometimes, it's not the law that changed the world, but the one that was never written."

Redlining wasn't declared law—it was woven into policies, quietly mapped, and enacted through routine lending practices. There was no official bill. No loud announcement. Just quietly drawn lines that shaped generations of inequality in housing and wealth. The law that was never written still shaped the world.

The Quiet Redline

It was never shouted from a podium. It didn't pass through Congress with fanfare or fiery debate. There was no press conference, no signature with a golden pen. Instead, it arrived quietly—penciled into maps, embedded into policies, disguised as procedure.

Redlining wasn't shouted; it was penciled—quietly marking futures without a sound.

In the 1930s, as America sought to stabilize its housing market, the federal government commissioned the Home Owners' Loan Corporation to assess risk in neighborhoods across the country. What they created were color-coded maps—green for "Best," blue for "Still Desirable," yellow for "Definitely Declining," and red for "Hazardous." But the criteria weren't based solely on economics or infrastructure—they were steeped in race.

"Injustice doesn't always arrive with noise. Sometimes, it hides in silence—tucked inside policies, disguised as neutral maps, and reinforced by decisions no one questions anymore."

Predominantly Black and immigrant neighborhoods, regardless of financial viability, were outlined in red. Labeled hazardous. Unworthy of investment. Not with a megaphone, but with a map.

Banks followed the lines. Loans were denied. Investment dried up. And what followed was a kind of slow erasure—communities starved of opportunity while others flourished next door.

This wasn't policy written in ink.

It was policy hidden in practice.

A silent segregation that didn't need a law to be legal.

In response to this injustice, the Fair Housing Act of 1968 emerged, aiming to dismantle the discriminatory practices that redlining perpetuated.

Yet, even as the law was signed, the quiet lines on the maps remained—an enduring legacy of inequality that would take generations to unravel.

Redlining wasn't shouted; it was penciled — quietly marking futures without a sound.

A study published in 2020 revealed that homes in Black neighborhoods are still undervalued compared to similar homes in white neighborhoods.

Not because of the homes themselves, but because of where they are.

The shadow of those old red lines stretches long, and we still haven't found the courage, or the political will, to redraw them.

And the truth is, this isn't just a housing issue.

It's a health issue.

An education issue.

An access issue.

It's a "who gets to dream" issue.

What makes redlining especially insidious is how ordinary it looked on paper.

Just a map.

Just a form.

Just a box checked or unchecked.

But in those quiet decisions, entire futures were shaped.

Generational wealth denied.

School systems underfunded.

Businesses unable to launch.

The American dream rewritten based on what side of the line you lived on.

It's a haunting reminder that injustice isn't always loud.

Sometimes it's bureaucratic.

Sometimes it's a "no" buried in paperwork.

Sometimes it's the policy that was never made explicit—because then no one could challenge it.

And yet, the impact was unmistakable.

Historical Insight

Redlining wasn't an act of ignorance; it was a decision made in detail.

A quiet exclusion.

A missed law that should have declared all citizens worthy of opportunity.

And like many injustices, its power came from its silence.

No alarms.

Just absence.

That's the danger of the unwritten: it escapes notice until the consequences are too big to ignore.

Modern Echoes: Redlining in the Digital Age

The lines may no longer be drawn on paper maps, but they still exist—etched now into algorithms, ZIP codes, and zoning boards.

Today's redlining wears different clothes: school district boundaries that reinforce segregation, mortgage approval algorithms that mirror historical bias, and even internet service deserts in low-income communities.

Redlining wasn't an act of ignorance; it was a decision made in detail.

The injustice has gone digital—but the impact is analog.

Lived. Felt.

Leadership Lens

I remember sitting in a leadership meeting a few years ago, reviewing site options for a new health clinic. The data felt sterile—demographics, traffic patterns, average income.

All of it looked neutral. Rational. Justifiable.

But then I asked,

"Where is the data not pointing us?"

"What would it mean to invest in the places the numbers quietly warn us to avoid—where the demographics suggest we don't belong?"

That single question shifted the room.

Because sometimes, data is just a polished record of past exclusion.

And if we're not paying attention, we'll follow it faithfully, replicating injustice, dressed up as strategy.

True leadership notices the invisible boundaries—and dares to cross them.

True leadership listens differently—it honors what was, sees what is, and owns what could be.

Redrawing the Lines – A Story of Legacy and Listening

The clinic in Cedar Lake, Indiana, began with a community needs assessment and a map. As we gathered for our annual board retreat, the atmosphere buzzed with anticipation. The smell of strong coffee and the sound of colored markers on flip charts filled the conference room, where we had cleared the day for strategy—big-picture thinking, whiteboards, and bold ideas. At the heart of the day's activities, our strategic pillars took center stage: Behavioral Health, Primary Care, Social Health, and Community First.

At the front of the room, a large video monitor displayed our data and a map of our service area. It illustrated demographics, population trends, and access-to-care ratios. The analytics team had done their work well. Cedar Lake was highlighted on the map, signaling an opportunity. "It's a strategic choice," I said, and the data indeed made sense. The spreadsheets told a story of growth and potential.

For over fifty years, Edgewater Health has served the community of Gary, Indiana—not as outsiders, but as steadfast partners. Our presence extends beyond clinics; we are woven into the fabric of homes, schools, churches, and the very hearts of the people we serve. As I reflect on our journey, I feel a profound weight in my heart. The numbers on the screen tell one story, but they fail to capture the true essence of Gary—a community just a short drive away yet perceived as a world apart.

Sometimes, data is just a polished record of past exclusion.

The data points show a market that has faced headwinds, with slower growth than desired. Decades of red lines—both literal and symbolic—shaped its past, but the story is far from over. Each decision made now has the power to influence what comes next. History may have drawn the lines, but the future will be defined by how we choose to cross them.

Edgewater Health has never been a numbers-only organization. We have weathered the storms of steel closures, stigma, and silence alongside this resilient community. We've stood shoulder to shoulder with its residents through industry collapse, population loss, racial disinvestment, and waves of political neglect. While Cedar Lake may have appeared on our maps, Gary's story is etched in our hearts, a narrative that cannot be measured merely by data points.

The clinic in Cedar Lake, Indiana, began with a community needs assessment and a map.

The data highlighted Cedar Lake as a strategic opportunity.

But Gary's story—the one not told by the spreadsheets—anchored our hearts.

For over fifty years, Edgewater Health had stood with Gary through collapse, neglect, and silence.

Cedar Lake became a model of what could be.

Gary remained our covenant of what must always be.

Opening the Cedar Lake clinic reminded us: Data tells one story. People tell another.

And when in doubt, we listen to the people.

The Lines We Don't See

Redlining didn't end with housing maps.

It continues anytime we let fear, familiarity, or financial comfort guide our choices.

The decision to go into Cedar Lake—and to stay rooted in Gary—wasn't just about expansion.

It was about redrawing the lines.

Strategy without soul is just motion.

As we continue to walk with Gary, we are committed to honoring its legacy.

Leadership isn't measured by how many new places we reach—it's measured by how faithfully we serve where we are rooted.

Redrawing the Story

The clinic in Cedar Lake wasn't a departure from our mission.

It was a reminder that the call to serve can echo from places both familiar and new.

Strategy without soul is just motion.

But our compass wasn't just data—it was legacy.

Gary is in our DNA.

And as we grow, we don't pivot away from that story—we carry it with us.

In the end, it wasn't the big decisions that defined this story—it was the quiet ones.

The overlooked map.

The unasked question.

The act of listening when data fell silent.

Because the future we long for isn't built in sweeping gestures.

It's built in the small things.

The details.

And in choosing to see what others overlook, we begin to redraw the world—not just with strategy, but with soul.

Because it's in the details: the small things that mean everything.

Soul Pause

Redrawing the Line

1. Where in your life or leadership are you relying on "data" that might be outdated or incomplete?
2. Have you ever avoided a place, a person, or a problem be cause it didn't "fit the model"?
3. What legacy are you upholding—and what boundaries might it be time to cross or redefine?

Action Invitation:

Choose one "quiet redline" in your world to challenge—whether it's a mindset, a map, or a moment of silence.

What small action can you take this week to redraw it with equity, empathy, or intention?

Remember:

The lines we challenge today shape the futures we cannot yet see.

When Maps Go Quiet

Not all boundaries are visible. Some are drawn in policy. Others are carved into perception.

The most dangerous ones, though, are the ones we stop seeing altogether. When we trust only the metrics, we miss the meaning.

When we follow the map but forget the mission, we risk losing our way.

The real challenge of leadership isn't just making decisions that make sense.

It's making decisions that make a difference.

Especially when the data is silent—and the need is still loud.

Final Reflection: The Details We Choose to See

Injustice rarely announces itself.

It creeps in through the maps we trust, the data we revere, and the silence we never question.

The story of redlining reminds us that leadership demands more than following numbers—it demands seeing the people behind them.

True impact isn't built only on strategies and spreadsheets.

It's built in the spaces between: the overlooked, the underestimated, the places and people easy to ignore.

In every decision, we choose which details to honor—and which stories to carry forward.

The world is redrawn every day, not by grand declarations, but by small acts of courage, empathy, and intention.

Because it's in the details—the ones we choose to see—that everything changes.

The Details Beneath

1. Redlining refers to the practice used by the Home Owners' Loan Corporation in the 1930s, which mapped urban areas and rated neighborhoods for mortgage risk—often ranking Black and immigrant communities as "hazardous" based solely on race.
2. These maps did not formally outlaw lending, but they heavily influenced banks and institutions, contributing to decades of disinvestment in communities of color.
3. The Fair Housing Act of 1968 sought to outlaw redlining, but studies show that its legacy persists in property values, school funding, and economic opportunity.
4. A 2020 Brookings report found that homes in majority-Black neighborhoods are appraised at significantly lower values than comparable homes in white neighborhoods.
5. Modern redlining also appears in data-driven decisions, such as credit scoring algorithms, zoning laws, and internet access disparities—all of which can reproduce historical injustices in new forms.
6. The story of Cedar Lake and Gary reflects how strategic planning must go beyond numbers to honor history, equity, and lived experience.

*Further reading and selected references for this chapter are available in the Notes & Sources section at the end of this book.

Small Moments Write the Story of Our Lives

Redacted Memory—The Quiet War on Truth

"The most dangerous lines are the ones we stop seeing—the ones drawn in silence, enforced by habit, and overlooked by history."
— Dr. Danita Johnson Woods

History does not always vanish in flames. Sometimes it fades in quiet decisions—a paragraph cut from a textbook, a name dropped from a lesson, a truth softened until it loses its edge.

This chapter is not just about what's been removed.

It's about what we've been taught not to miss.

What happens when the record skips over your name, your struggle, your triumph, your pain?

What happens when the story of a nation leaves its own people out?

This is the war most don't see.

Not fought with guns or tanks, but with red pens, closed doors, and silent approvals.

And like all wars, it leaves casualties, memory, identity, justice, and truth.

CHAPTER NINETEEN

Redacted Memory—The Quiet War on Truth

"Erasure is not silence—it is strategy. And history's edits always have an agenda."
— Dr. Danita Johnson Woods

When a Story is Stripped

Not all erasure is violent Sometimes, it's as small as a missing line. A word left out. A story untold. A chapter quietly skipped.

At first, it feels like nothing. The book is still bound. The lesson still taught. The page is still there—just lighter. Thinner. Less alive.

But truth doesn't disappear because you stop telling it. It disappears because you stop noticing it missing.

When we lose the details, we lose the truth. And when we lose the truth, we lose our footing as a people.

Erasure isn't a mistake. It's a method. A method of control. A method of forgetting. A method of shaping the future by rewriting the past.

Every detail erased is a thread pulled loose from the fabric of democracy itself. And what unravels in silence can take generations to repair. Because every small omission—every missing name, every softened phrase, every redacted paragraph—tells the next generation what they're allowed to remember.

Erasure isn't a mistake. It's a method.

When we erase the details, we erase the inheritance of resilience, too. And a nation without memory becomes a nation without direction.

It's in the details—what's named, what's omitted—that a people's true story either survives or slowly slips away.

The Student Who Didn't See Herself

Nia was ten years old the first time she noticed the absence.

Her fifth-grade class was beginning a unit on American history. She flipped through the pages of the textbook with curiosity, eager to learn about the people who built the country.

There were pictures of Founding Fathers, battlefields, tall ships, and declarations.

But no one looked like her.

There were no stories of Harriet or Ida or Fannie. No mention of Tulsa. No diagrams of slave ships. No photographs of lunch counter sit-ins or school integration.

There was a sentence—just one—that said enslaved Africans "worked on plantations" and were "treated unfairly."

Treated unfairly?

Nia didn't have the language yet for what was wrong. But she felt it—deep in her chest.

It wasn't just what was said.

It was what wasn't said.

It was the quiet removal of pain, of power, of people.

And when she raised her hand to ask a question, her teacher shifted uncomfortably, then moved on.

At home, Nia's mother handed her a different book. It was worn, pages marked, stories raw. It told the truth—and it made Nia cry.

But it also made her proud. Because for the first time, she saw the strength of her people. The resistance. The brilliance. The contribution.

Truth doesn't disappear because you stop telling it.

She saw herself. And she realized: The absence was not an accident. It was a decision made in boardrooms, school districts, and publishing houses.

A detail dismissed here. A chapter omitted there. A nation shaped not only by what it remembers, but by what it chooses to forget. That day, Nia began to understand that history isn't just about facts—it's about framing. And when you erase the details, you erase the people.

But she also learned something else: That reclaiming the truth doesn't start with a whole library. It starts with one book. One question. One brave voice refusing to look away.

Erasure Is a Tool of Control

This is why the banning of books matters.

It is not about protecting innocence—it is about preserving ignorance.

And ignorance is fertile ground for injustice.

When we decide children are "too young" to learn about racism, but not too young to experience it—

When we treat the truth as "too political" for the classroom, but allow fear and falsehoods to fester—

When we remove voices from the curriculum because they are too bold, too Black, too queer, too complicated—

We are not keeping students safe. We are keeping them uninformed.

You cannot teach democracy and redact its cost. And uninformed citizens cannot preserve a democracy. They cannot fight for freedom they never knew was at risk. They cannot speak up for injustice they were taught never happened. They cannot change systems they were told don't exist.

This is not just about books. It's about legacy. It's about who gets remembered—and who gets erased. It's about which truths survive, and which lies we build upon.

It's about the details. Because in the details, democracy either breathes—or it withers.

Perspective: Why Civic Memory Matters

Civic memory is the heartbeat of democracy.

It's the way a nation remembers itself—the good, the brutal, the unfinished.

> ***You cannot teach democracy and redact its cost.***

When history is told in full, a people rise in resilience.

When history is trimmed and tailored, a people forget their fight—and lose their future.

Why it matters:

- Memory builds accountability. Forgetting builds apathy.
- Memory fuels courage. Forgetting breeds complacency.
- Memory binds us to justice. Forgetting binds us to comfort.

Protecting civic memory is not about guilt.

It's about responsibility. Because we cannot heal what we refuse to name.

Civic memory is the heartbeat of democracy.

Soul Pause

The Stories We Hold

Take a breath.
Turn inward.
Reflect.

1. Ask yourself:

- *What truths was I taught—and what truths were missing entirely?*
- *Whose voices shaped my understanding of history?*
- *Who helped me see the parts others tried to erase?*
- *Where do I now feel called to tell the truth, even if it is uncomfortable?*

2. Now go deeper:

- *How can I help protect access to full, truthful education in my community?*
- *What conversations have I been avoiding because they might cause discomfort?*
- *How will I stay rooted in truth when it would be easier—and safer—to look away?*

Because remembering is not passive. It's a practice.

And practicing truth—over and over—is how we keep freedom alive.

What's Happening Now—It's Not Just the Books. It's the Blueprint.

Erasure today doesn't come with burning crosses or banned marches. It comes with policies tucked into late-night school board meetings. It comes with sanitized curriculum laws written to sound neutral. It comes with slow, surgical strikes against the truth—disguised as "parental rights" or "academic standards."

Book bans are spreading across dozens of states. Titles pulled because they name racism too clearly or affirm LGBTQ+ students too boldly. Libraries defunded. Educators threatened. Students left with half-truths and empty pages.

At the same time, Diversity, Equity, and Inclusion (DEI) programs are being dismantled. Funding slashed. Departments closed. Critical race theory reduced to a political football few have actually read.

This is not random. It's coordinated. It's a blueprint for forgetting.

Erase the hard history. Deny the systemic barriers. Teach a generation to stop asking hard questions—and the systems of power remain untouched.

It's not just the books. It's the future being rewritten, detail by missing detail.

And the most dangerous part? The change feels small enough that many won't notice until it's too late.

Because that's how erasure wins: Not with a roar.

But with a quiet edit.

Final Reflection: Why the Details Still Matter

This isn't just a chapter about book bans. It's about who we choose to be as a people.

It's about whether we build a nation on half-truths and redacted memories—or on a full reckoning with the messy, magnificent, painful story we actually lived.

When we lose the details, we lose the map. When we erase the names, the movements, the betrayals, the bravery—we lose the compass that keeps democracy alive.

Because the truth doesn't just teach us what happened. It teaches us what must never happen again.

Every small omission—every missing paragraph, every banned book, every whitewashed lesson—is not an isolated act. It's a slow rewriting of the future.

History is not lost in grand battles alone. It's lost in the tiny edits we decide not to notice.

That's why every detail matters.

Because the smallest lines—left in or left out—shape who we become next.

And when we guard the details, we guard the dream.

The Details Beneath

1. "What we forget, we are doomed to repeat." While often paraphrased, this concept originates from George Santayana's 1905 work *The Life of Reason: The Phases of Human Progress.*

2. Nia's story is a composite, drawn from real accounts of students responding to sanitized curricula.

3. In the mid-2020s, many state legislatures moved to restrict DEI initiatives in education and government, a pattern that may evolve but reflects long-running conflicts over race, rights, and power.

*Further reading and selected references for this chapter are available in the Notes & Sources section at the end of this book.

The Memory We Inherit: How Civic Memory Shapes Democracy

"The stories we choose to remember—or forget—
become the blueprints for the world we build."
— Dr. Danita Johnson Woods

It begins quietly; in the spaces we rarely notice. A statue in a town square. A chapter in a history book. A plaque tucked onto the side of an old courthouse. A holiday we celebrate—or one we quietly ignore.

Together, these fragments form something far greater than individual memories: they build our civic memory, the collective story of who we believe we are, what we value, and where we believe we come from.

And like any blueprint, this memory shapes what comes next.

When certain stories are elevated and others are erased, democracy itself begins to tilt, favoring the myths we prefer over the truths we must confront.

When history is curated for comfort instead of courage, our collective future narrows.

Every small decision about what we preserve, teach, and honor feeds into the soil of citizenship.

Civic memory is not just a recollection of the past—it is an inheritance, a foundation, and a responsibility.

The health of our democracy depends on how honestly and how bravely we tend to it.

CHAPTER TWENTY

The Memory We Inherit: How Civic Memory Shapes Democracy

"Civic memory is not nostalgia—it is a mirror. And what we see in it depends on what we choose to remember."
— Dr. Danita Johnson Woods

Civic memory is a society's collective remembrance of its past, especially as it relates to public life, democracy, justice, and national identity. It's how we remember (or forget) the events, people, movements, and decisions that shape our country—and how those memories influence our policies, values, and sense of belonging today.

It Was Just a Statue

At least, that's what I thought the first time I really noticed it—tall, stoic, cast in bronze, standing in the middle of a public plaza I had walked through more times than I could count. His name was etched into the base in capital letters, but I never stopped to read it. I passed him on my way to lunch, to city meetings, to community events. He was part of the background—unchanging, unchallenged.

Until one day, I paused. I looked him up. And what I found stunned me. He wasn't a statesman or civil rights icon. He was a Confederate general—a man who fought to preserve slavery. A man whose likeness had been placed on public land, not by accident, but by design. It was meant to send a message—about who mattered, and who didn't.

That statue had stood there longer than I'd been alive. And I had never really seen it. Never questioned it. But once I did, I couldn't unsee it.

It made me wonder:

What else have we inherited without ever examining?

What other stories shape our civic memory—not because they were true, but because they were repeated?

Civic memory isn't always built through conscious choice. Sometimes, it's absorbed through what we're told to honor—and what we're trained to overlook. In this chapter, we trace how small markers—plaques, street names, monuments—quietly narrate our public story. And what happens when we start to read them for ourselves.

The Power of What We Preserve

Civic memory is the story we tell about ourselves—not in journals or textbooks alone, but in public spaces, school names, holidays, statues, and maps. It's the difference between a plaque and a paragraph. Between what we preserve with granite and what we edit with silence.

We often think history is in the past, but civic memory shows us: it's everywhere, right now.

We haven't forgotten history—we've just remembered it selectively.

And the details—what we choose to commemorate, whose names we give to buildings, whose faces we chisel in stone—tell us who we are and what we value. Or what we are still afraid to confront.

***The stories we choose to remember—or forget—
become the blueprints for the world we build.***

When you start paying attention, it becomes clear: We've remembered the generals but forgotten the enslaved. We've honored founding fathers but left out founding mothers. We've painted freedom in red, white, and blue—but left no space for Black and brown truth.

And just like that, one decision—one statue, one renaming, one erasure—becomes a blueprint for how future generations understand their place in this country.

Reflections That Shape a Nation

In cities across America, this reckoning is still playing out in real time. Statues are coming down—not to erase history, but to correct the memory. Schools are being renamed to honor educators, innovators, and activists instead of oppressors. New memorials and museums are being built—not to glorify power, but to tell the truth about its consequences.

Yet, alongside these steps forward, there is resistance. Movements—fueled in part by the MAGA era—push to halt or reverse these changes. Book bans, curriculum restrictions, and challenges to inclusive education have become battlegrounds over who gets to shape the nation's story.

These are not just symbolic acts. They are declarations of value. Of visibility. Of legacy. And they remind us that democracy does not live only in laws—it lives in memory. Resistance doesn't erase the truth—it makes the fight to preserve it even more urgent.

The Backlash to Remembering

And just as swiftly as the reckoning came, a quiet reversal began to take its place.

In the months following that painful summer—the marches, the murals, the memorials—it felt, for a moment, as though the nation had paused to see itself clearly. Corporations issued public commitments to racial equity. School districts examined long-ignored gaps in curriculum. DEI offices opened. Statues came down. There was a sense—fragile, but real—that the stories we tell and the truths we face might finally begin to shift.

But memory, especially honest memory, has always had its enemies.

Today, across the country, we are witnessing a coordinated retreat. DEI programs are not just being questioned, they're being dismantled. Books are not just being challenged, they're banned. Not because they lie, but because they tell the truth too plainly. Curricula are being rewritten to sidestep discomfort. And policies once created to repair harm are being recast as threats to unity.

When we forget the hard truths, we forfeit the power to shape what comes next.

The language of justice is being rebranded as divisive. The pursuit of equity is being painted as extremism. The very tools designed to help us reckon with our past are being stripped away—quietly, but deliberately.

It feels, at times, like we're being asked not to remember too loudly.

To accept a version of history that demands nothing.

To move on from wounds that were never allowed to heal.

But civic memory isn't meant to comfort. It is meant to clarify.

It doesn't exist to protect our pride—it exists to protect our progress.

Because when we stop telling the full truth about where we've been, we start surrendering the power to shape where we're going.

And the moment we stop asking hard questions about our past, we begin losing control of our future.

This isn't just a cultural shift. It's a moral one.

And every statue left standing, every book pulled from a shelf, every untaught truth becomes part of the memory we pass down.

Democracy is not just governed by rules—it is rooted in remembrance.

Because when we erase the difficult parts of our past, we weaken the foundation of our future. And when we remember—fully, honestly, even painfully— we open the door to healing, accountability, and real progress.

And just as the story of redlining teaches us, what is left out of the record shapes the present just as powerfully as what is written in it.

What We Remember—and What We Don't

Tulsa: A City Buried Twice

For decades, the name "Tulsa" meant little more to most Americans than a city in Oklahoma. But for the descendants of Greenwood—once known as Black Wall Street—it meant loss, legacy, and a silence too loud to bear.

In 1921, a prosperous Black community was burned to the ground in one of the worst acts of racial violence in U.S. history. Over 35 square blocks were destroyed. More than 300 people killed. Thousands displaced. The attack was organized, brutal, and state sanctioned.

And then it vanished from public record.

For nearly a century, the Tulsa Race Massacre was not taught in Oklahoma schools. Entire generations grew up without knowing it happened—even those whose ancestors had lived through it. It wasn't in textbooks. It wasn't in museum exhibits. It wasn't in the civic memory of the city. It was a wound without a name.

Only in recent years—through survivor testimony, investigative journalism, and the relentless work of community historians—has the story begun to reemerge. Statues and historical markers now try to piece together what was broken. But the damage of deliberate forgetting still lingers.

> ***Freedom isn't just something you grant. It's something you have to remember—and fight to preserve.***

Juneteenth: The Freedom We Forgot

When Juneteenth became a federal holiday in 2021, many Americans celebrated with pride. But for others, especially Black communities in Texas and beyond, the day had been sacred for generations.

June 19, 1865, marks the day Union soldiers arrived in Galveston, Texas, and finally enforced the Emancipation Proclamation—two and a half years after it was signed. For the last enslaved people in the Confederacy, it was the first taste of freedom.

So why did it take 156 years to recognize it nationally?

Because freedom isn't just something you grant. It's something you have to remember—and fight to preserve. And until recently, Juneteenth was excluded from national civic memory. Schools didn't teach it. Calendars didn't mark it. Federal buildings didn't close for it.

But the celebration never stopped in the hearts of those who remembered.

It's a reminder that even when a country forgets, a community can still hold the memory close—until it becomes impossible to ignore.

> ***"Memory is not neutral. It either affirms dignity or denies it."***

The Statue Still Standing

In a Southern town not unlike many others, a Confederate statue stands watch over the county courthouse. Erected decades after the Civil War—not to honor the dead, but to intimidate the living. During Jim Crow. During segregation. A not-so-subtle reminder of who held power and whose rights were conditional.

Activists have fought for years to have it removed. But local leaders insist it's "a part of history."

They're right. It is.

But the question isn't whether it's history, it's which history we choose to honor.

Memory is not neutral. It either affirms dignity or denies it. Because civic memory doesn't just happen. It's curated. Voted on. Budgeted. Etched into stone. And that statue—standing tall on taxpayer-funded ground—is a reminder that sometimes the past isn't past at all.

It's present. And very much alive.

Soul Pause

What Am I Walking Past?

This week, pay close attention to the spaces you move through. Look for:

1. Names on buildings
2. Statues in the park
3. Signs outside schools
4. Murals, plaques, or historical markers

Then reflect:

1. *What do these symbols say about your community's values?*
2. *Whose stories are being celebrated? Whose are missing?*
3. *What did you see today that you've never really noticed before?*
4. *What role do I play in shaping the memory of my community?*
5. *What story do I want to make sure is never forgotten?*

Democracy isn't sustained by speeches. It's protected by memory.

Civic Memory in Everyday Life

The History That Hangs in the Air

Civic memory isn't just in museums, it's in the everyday. It's in:

- Street signs and building names
- Which holidays are observed—and which are ignored
- Whose portraits hang in schools, hospitals, or city halls
- What plaques say (or don't say) on public land
- How cities mark "history" vs. "tragedy"

These details send messages. Even when we don't notice them consciously, they shape what we believe about power, belonging, and truth.

Civic memory teaches us not just what happened—but who mattered.

Start noticing. Ask questions. Be curious. Because the past is present. And the present is choosing what the future will remember.

Final Reflection: The Details That Shape Democracy

Civic memory is not just about what we remember, it's about how we choose to live in that remembrance. It's about whether we inherit a nation built on myth, or one willing to tell the truth.

And right now, that choice is being tested.

Because just as quickly as truths were uncovered, some are now being buried again. The temptation to sanitize, to simplify, to forget is real. But every name we restore, every story we teach, every monument we question, becomes an act of resistance against forgetting.

When we change a name, teach a buried story, or take down a monument that never should've stood, we aren't erasing history—we're correcting the memory. We're restoring the dignity that silence tried to steal.

In the end, democracy is not sustained by grand speeches or sweeping gestures. It is protected by what we choose to notice. And the smallest of those choices—what we teach, what we rename, what we honor—are the details that shape the soul of a nation.

The Details Beneath

1. The statue anecdote in this chapter serves as a composite story, reflecting real experiences across many American towns and cities where Confederate monuments have remained in public spaces without question for decades.

2. Civic memory refers to the way a society collectively remembers its past, especially in public, symbolic, and institutional ways. It influences identity, belonging, and the shaping of future policies.

3. The Tulsa Race Massacre was not widely taught in American schools until recent decades. Survivors' testimonies and efforts by journalists and historians helped bring the story back into public awareness.

4. Juneteenth was celebrated for generations in Black communities before being recognized as a federal holiday in 2021. The delay speaks to the ways Black freedom narratives were often excluded from mainstream civic memory.

5. DEI (Diversity, Equity, and Inclusion) programs have faced increasing pushback in recent years, with legislation, litigation, and political movements challenging their presence in education, healthcare, and corporate spaces.

*Further reading and selected references for this chapter are available in the Notes & Sources section at the end of this book.

Small Moments Write the Story of Our Lives

A Lens on Little Things: Stories that Shift the World

"Sometimes, the only difference between being seen and being forgotten is the pause someone was willing to take."
— Dr. Danita Johnson Woods

We are surrounded by stories we never hear. They pass us on sidewalks, sit behind us on buses, and stand silently in checkout lines. Not because they have nothing to say—but because we rarely stop long enough to ask.

Sometimes, the loudest impact comes from the smallest gesture: a question asked with sincerity, a pause held with patience, a gaze that lingers long enough to truly see. These are the moments that invite us into another person's world—not to fix, judge, or define, but simply to witness.

This chapter is about those small, sacred invitations. The ones that turn passersby into storytellers. The ones that remind us that attention is not just kindness, —it is power. And it is through that lens, sharpened by silence and shaped by curiosity, that we find the threads connecting us all.

CHAPTER TWENTY-ONE

A Lens on Little Things: Stories that Shift the World

It's in the silence between words that humanity often speaks the loudest.
— Dr. Danita Johnson Woods

What is one small story from your life that, if someone asked the right question, would reveal something beautiful, brave, or broken in you?

The Power of the Pause: Brandon Stanton and the Stories We Walk Past

I used to believe that changing the world required a microphone, a movement, or at least a boardroom full of strategy. But over time, I've come to understand something quieter and more profound: sometimes, all it takes is a question—and the courage to truly listen. Brandon Stanton's Humans of New York taught me that. His lens doesn't just capture faces; it captures moments we usually rush past. The quiet pause before a confession. The tremble in a hand that's trying to be brave. The detail that everyone else missed.

Brandon Stanton wasn't setting out to change the world. He just wanted to photograph people—real people. The kind you pass on the street without a second glance. A security guard on break. A grandmother at the bus stop. A child holding a balloon. He started Humans of New York with a simple premise: take portraits of everyday New

Yorkers and pair them with quotes from short conversations. But what emerged from this small, consistent act was something far more profound—a global movement of empathy, awareness, and intimate storytelling.

Over time, the captions grew longer, and the questions became deeper. And in the quiet spaces between a stranger's sentence, the world leaned in to listen.

The most powerful stories are the ones we almost didn't hear.

What made Humans of New York extraordinary wasn't just the photography. It was Brandon's attention to detail—his ability to catch the hesitation in a voice, the flicker of pain in an eye, the story hiding behind a smile. These weren't headlines or curated bios. These were fragments of truth. And in sharing them, Brandon reminded us of something we often forget in our hurried lives: everyone carries a story, and sometimes, the smallest invitation to share it can bring healing, hope, or justice.

And indeed, some stories changed lives—and systems.

When a young boy named Vidal shared that his principal was the person who "tells us we matter," Brandon followed the thread. He profiled Mott Hall Bridges Academy in Brownsville, Brooklyn, and its visionary leader, Principal Nadia Lopez. The story, published in January 2015, went viral. Within days, more than $1.4 million was raised—enough to send hundreds of students on college visits and establish a scholarship fund. The story made national headlines, and its reach stretched all the way to the White House, where Vidal and Principal Lopez were invited to meet President Barack Obama (New York Times, Jan. 2015).

Change didn't begin with a protest or a platform—it began with a question.

In Bangladesh, Brandon met Dr. Zaki Haider, a pediatric oncologist with a dream of building the country's first children's cancer hospital. After sharing the story in February 2016, readers donated over $2 million to help make the dream a reality (HONY, February 2016).

He also traveled to Pakistan and told the story of Syeda Ghulam Fatima, a woman leading the fight to end bonded labor in brick kilns. Her post, published in October 2015, led to more than $2 million in donations, which helped free enslaved workers and expand her mission (BBC News, October 2015).

Then came the story of a Syrian refugee family. Brandon documented their journey with raw, personal accounts in September 2015. The emotional response was swift and global, raising more than $750,000 to support the family's resettlement and aid other displaced families (CNN, Sept. 2015).

Small questions. Honest answers. Global impact.

These weren't campaigns born in boardrooms. They were born from conversations. From details. From noticing the ache behind a word and giving it a platform.

Brandon has also spoken directly to public discourse. In March 2016, he wrote an open letter on Facebook addressed to then-presidential candidate Donald Trump. The letter sharply criticized Trump's rhetoric around immigrants, Muslims, and marginalized communities. It became one of the most shared posts in Humans of New York history, reaching millions (New York Post, March 2016).

You don't need a stage to change the world. Sometimes, all you need is a camera and the courage to ask.

That's the power of detail. The power of pausing long enough to truly see someone.

Brandon didn't build a nonprofit empire or run for office. He simply listened. He asked better questions. And he helped the world do the same.

Attention is the currency of compassion.

It's in the details—the careful listening, the patient questions, the refusal to reduce someone to a label or statistic. That's what changes everything.

Soul Pause

The Sacred Power of Paying Attention

In a world of noise, paying attention is an act of love. For one day, resist the urge to scroll past. To brush off. To interrupt. Instead, pause and become a witness.

1. Make eye contact with the person bagging your groceries.
2. Ask someone, "How are you really?"—and wait for the answer.
3. Look up from your phone and into the world.
   Notice what shifts—not just in them, but in you.

Sometimes, the most meaningful change begins with a question and a quiet willingness to hear the truth.

Everyone has a story. Most are just waiting for someone to ask.

Journal Moment: The Story I Almost Missed

Think of a time you overlooked someone—or were overlooked.

Now reflect:

1. *What did you assume? What details did you miss?*
2. *How might the story have changed if you had paused, asked, or listened more deeply?*
3. *Who in your life might be carrying an untold story right now?*

Now flip the lens:

When was the last time someone truly saw you? What did they notice that others didn't?

Write freely. Don't rush the reflection. The smallest moment may hold your greatest revelation.

How to Use Your Platform with Purpose

- Treat your platform like a borrowed microphone: speak for yourself, but make room for voices people rarely hand the mic to in the first place.
- Lead with listening, not lessons: before you post, ask, "What am I truly hearing from this person or community, and am I honoring that?"
- Tell stories that move people, not just move metrics: if a post gets attention but doesn't deepen empathy or understanding, it's just noise.

- Protect people's dignity in every detail: if someone trusts you with their story, your first job is their safety and humanity, not your content calendar.
- Use your reach to circulate resources, not just feelings: when a story exposes a need, pair it with a tangible next step—an organization, a phone call, a way to show up

---

Reflection Prayer

The Courage to Witness

God of truth and justice,
Give me eyes that do not look away.
Give me hands that hold the sacred weight of story.
Give me a heart that is tender enough to care,
and strong enough to act.
May my voice be a light in dark spaces.
May my platform be a place of refuge, truth, and freedom.
May I never underestimate the power of one post,
one prayer, one spark.
Let me be found faithful—not just in what I say,
but in what I choose to see.
Amen.

— Dr. Danita Johnson Woods

Final Reflection: The Sacred Act of Seeing

The stories that Brandon Stanton captures remind us that small things, when seen, have the power to heal, to connect, and even to save. But what about the things we don't see? The moments when no one asked the question, when no one paid attention, when a letter went unread or a law remained unwritten? If a photograph can reveal a soul, then what happens when no one is there to take the picture? What happens when the detail is missed entirely?

History has repeatedly answered that question—with revolutions that started from overlooked notes, wars that could have been avoided with a single message sent on time, or justice that slipped through the cracks of forgotten paperwork. Sometimes, it's not what we do, but what we don't do, that changes everything.

The Details Beneath

1. The story of Vidal and Principal Lopez, featured on Humans of New York, demonstrated how a single interview can generate national momentum and financial support for under-resourced schools.

2. Brandon Stanton's storytelling and global donor response significantly advanced Dr. Zaki Haider's dream of building a children's cancer hospital in Bangladesh.

3. Syeda Ghulam Fatima's work against bonded labor in Pakistan gained international attention and funding after being profiled by Humans of New York.

4. Brandon Stanton's open letter to Donald Trump exemplified how storytelling platforms can also serve as vehicles for political critique and public discourse.

5. This chapter underscores how empathetic attention—the act of truly noticing people—can influence systems, reshape narratives, and catalyze justice.

*Further reading and selected references for this chapter are available in the Notes & Sources section at the end of this book.

Small Moments Write the Story of Our Lives

Legacy: What Will They Remember?

"The legacy we leave is not just in our words or deeds, but in the hearts we touch and the lives we inspire."
— Unknown

Legacy often sounds like a grand concept—something reserved for presidents, poets, or people with statues in the town square. But legacy doesn't wait for eulogies or history books. It's being written right now, in the quiet choices we make and how we show up for others every day.

It's the teacher who stays late to help a struggling student. The grandmother whose recipes and wisdom live on at every family table. The mentor who sees possibility in someone the world has overlooked. These aren't headlines. They're handprints—left on hearts, not on paper.

The truth is that legacy isn't about being remembered by everyone. It's about being unforgettable to someone.

In this chapter, we pause to reflect on what we leave behind—not just in what we accomplish, but in how we love, how we lead, and how we live. Because it's in the smallest acts of intention that the biggest stories take root.

CHAPTER TWENTY-TWO

Legacy: What Will They Remember?

"Legacy isn't the echo of our name—it's the imprint of our love on someone else's life."
— Dr. Danita Johnson Woods

In 2014, the world was captivated by the passing of a remarkable woman: Maya Angelou. Her words had echoed through generations—poetry that breathed life into courage, stories that stitched together the broken parts of history, and a spirit that carried both fierce resistance and radical love. As she left this world at the age of 86, her legacy was felt far and wide—not just in literary halls and civil rights archives, but in the hearts of everyday people who had found strength in her voice.

Maya's legacy was not only written in books or engraved on plaques. It lived in the small, everyday moments that defined her character. She once said, "I've learned that people will forget what you said, people will forget what you did, but people will never forget how you made them feel."

Those words weren't theory for her. They were practice. Maya took the time to connect—to really see people, to hear their stories, to affirm their humanity whether through a poetry reading, a speech, or a passing conversation.

She reminds us that legacy is not built by sweeping gestures or grand pronouncements. It is crafted in the details of how we live, love, and lead. It grows in the small spaces: a listening ear, a word of encouragement, a brave act of truth-telling when silence would have been easier.

As we reflect on her life, a deeper question emerges:

What will they remember about us?

Every day, whether we recognize it or not, we are writing the story that others will tell about us. Legacy isn't some far-off epilogue at the end of a grand life—it is the fabric of our daily choices, woven together moment by moment. It's in the details.

Legacy isn't about being remembered by everyone.
It's about being unforgettable to someone.

And so, the question becomes not if we are leaving a legacy, but how.

Legacy is found in intention—the quiet decision to live as though every interaction matters. Malala Yousafzai, still just a girl when she stood up for the right to education, didn't set out to become a global icon. She simply knew that silence would betray everything she believed in. Her courage, rooted in small daily acts of resistance and persistence, built a legacy stretching across continents.

Legacy is found in how we love. In the way we hold space for others, offer grace in hard moments, or extend kindness without expecting a return. Mother Teresa of Calcutta didn't change the world through grand speeches. She did it by holding the hands of the dying, feeding the hungry, and lifting the forgotten. She lived her own words: *"Not all of us can do great things. But we can do small things with great love."*

Legacy is found in leadership that chooses service over status. Nelson Mandela, after decades of unjust imprisonment, chose reconciliation over revenge. His legacy was not just political; it was deeply human—a testament to how compassion, even when hard, can rebuild broken nations.

Legacy is found in the quiet courage of everyday people. Rosa Parks, refusing to give up her seat, likely did not imagine she would spark a movement. But her small act of defiance rewrote the story of American civil rights.

And legacy is found in us.

In the teachers who take an extra moment to encourage a struggling student.

In the volunteers who show up when no one is watching.

In the neighbor who checks in, the mentor who believes, the friend who listens without judgment.

These everyday actions ripple outward, shaping lives in ways we may never fully see.

The truth is, our actions extend far beyond the moment. A smile, a conversation, a choice to be kind—they can create ripples that reach generations. A child treated with dignity may grow up to extend dignity to thousands. A small word of encouragement can change the direction of a life.

When we pause to reflect, we must ask ourselves:

1. *What seeds am I planting today, whether or not I live to see them bloom?*

2. *How do I want to be remembered—not just by the world, but by the people closest to me?*

3. *Am I living each day with the same care I would hope to be remembered with?*

Crafting a meaningful legacy isn't about perfection. It isn't about fame.

It's about presence.

It's about consistency.

It's about the courage to believe that small things, done with great love, can change everything.

In the end, it won't be our titles or trophies that matter most.

It will be the people we loved, the moments we showed up, and the kindness we extended when it wasn't convenient.

Our legacy is being written right now—one choice, one conversation, one act of courage at a time.

Let it be a story worth remembering.

The truth is, our actions extend far beyond the moment.

The Legacy You're Living Now

Take a breath.

Slow down the urgency to achieve, and ask instead:

1. *Who will remember the kindness I offered when no one was looking?*
2. *Where have I planted seeds of courage, even if they haven't yet bloomed?*

3. *What silent example am I setting for the people who are watching without my knowledge?*
4. *How might small acts I make today echo in lives I'll never see?*

Your legacy isn't a someday project. It's already unfolding—quietly, beautifully—in how you move through the world.

Pause. Reflect. Live today in a way your future self would be proud to be remembered.

Small Acts That Build a Lasting Legacy

The Quiet Power of Action

- A note of encouragement can stay tucked in someone's heart for a lifetime.
- A brave "yes" or a firm "no" can realign a life's direction.
- An apology offered can heal generations of silent wounds.

Everyday Presence

- A steady presence during a storm can become someone's anchor.
- A small kindness may be the spark that reignites another's hope.
- In every room you exit, ask yourself: Did I leave grace here?

Intentional Leadership

- Speak Life: Words linger longer than you think. Speak encouragement, even when it feels small.
- Be Present: Your attention is more valuable than your advice. Give it generously.
- Honor Promises: The small promises we keep—or break—become the trust others remember.
- Uplift the Hidden: Notice and elevate the overlooked—a shy colleague, a tired server, a struggling student.

Legacy isn't left at the end of the journey.

It's sewn into every small act of love, truth, and presence along the way.

Final Reflection: What Will They Remember?

You will not be remembered only by what you built, but by what you touched.

Not only by what you conquered, but by what you cared for.

Not only by what you achieved, but by how you loved.

The smallest details—the moments that seem invisible—are the ones that will endure in the hearts of others. They will carry forward your tenderness, your truth, your courage.

Your story is being written in the quiet minutes between the milestones. Let every small act bear witness to the life you hoped to live.

Because it is in the details that small things change everything.

The Details Beneath

1. Maya Angelou's widely quoted reflection on memory and emotion underscores how legacy is often felt more than recorded.
2. Malala Yousafzai's advocacy began with a personal blog and evolved into a global movement, reminding us how small acts of courage shape global conversations.
3. Mother Teresa's legacy, rooted in compassion, illustrates how small acts of love can transcend cultural and religious boundaries.
4. Nelson Mandela's commitment to reconciliation over revenge transformed South Africa's post-apartheid journey and left a blueprint for restorative leadership.
5. Rosa Parks' decision not to give up her seat sparked the Montgomery Bus Boycott and catalyzed the modern civil rights movement in America.

*Further reading and selected references for this chapter are available in the Notes & Sources section at the end of this book.

Small Moments Write the Story of Our Lives

Notes & Sources: A Chapter-by-Chapter Reference

"Behind every insight is a trail of inquiry.
Here's where that trail begins."
— Dr. Danita Johnson Woods

Chapter 1: The Quiet Power of What's Often Overlooked

Further Reading

- Bryant, F. B., & Veroff, J. (2007). Savoring: A New Model of Positive Experience. Lawrence Erlbaum Associates Publishers. Wikipedia
- Kaufman, S. B., & Gregoire, C. (2015). Wired to Create: Unraveling the Mysteries of the Creative Mind. Perigee Books.
- McCullough, M. E., & Emmons, R. A. (2003). Counting blessings versus burdens: An experimental investigation of gratitude and subjective well-being in daily life. Journal of Personality and Social Psychology, 84(2), 377–389.Wikipedia
- Seligman, M. E. P. (2011). Flourish: A Visionary New Understanding of Happiness and Well-being. Free Press.
- Siegel, D. J. (2010). The Mindful Therapist: A Clinician's Guide to Mindsight and Neural Integration. W. W. Norton & Company.

Chapter 2: The Wolf and the Bee — Small Actions, Big Impact

Further Reading

- Food and Agriculture Organization of the United Nations. (2023). *Why Bees Matter*. https://www.fao.org/
- Lorenz, E. N. (1963). "Deterministic Nonperiodic Flow." *Journal of the Atmospheric Sciences*, 20(2), 130–141.
- Klein, A. M., et al. (2007). "Importance of pollinators in changing landscapes for world crops." *Proceedings of the Royal Society B: Biological Sciences*, 274(1608), 303–313.

Chapter 3: Life is a Mosaic

Further Reading

- BrainFacts.org. (2023). Neuroscience and Habits. https://www.brainfacts.org
- Graybiel, A. M. (2008). Habits, rituals, and the evaluative brain. Annual Review of Neuroscience, 31, 359–387. https://doi.org/10.1146/annurev.neuro.29.051605.112851
- Siegel, D. J. (2020). The Developing Mind: How Relationships and the Brain Interact to Shape Who We Are (3rd ed.). Guilford Press.
- Amabile, T., & Kramer, S. (2011). The power of small wins. Harvard Business Review. https://hbr.org/2011/05/the-power-of-small-wins
- Baumeister, R. F., & Tierney, J. (2011). Willpower: Rediscovering the Greatest Human Strength. Penguin Books.
- McAdams, D. P. (2006). The redemptive self: Generativity and the stories Americans live by. Research in Human Development, 3(2–3), 81–100. https://doi.org/10.1207/s15427617rhd0302_1

Chapter 4: Emotional Echoes—The Domino Effect

Further Reading

- Siegel, D. J., & Bryson, T. P. (2011). The Whole-Brain Child: 12 Revolutionary Strategies to Nurture Your Child's Developing Mind. New York: Bantam.
- Perry, B. D., & Szalavitz, M. (2017). The Boy Who Was Raised as a Dog: And Other Stories from a Child Psychiatrist's Notebook. New York: Basic Books.
- Doidge, N. (2007). The Brain That Changes Itself: Stories of Personal Triumph from the Frontiers of Brain Science. New York: Penguin.
- Fowler, J. H., & Christakis, N. A. (2010). Cooperative behavior cascades in human social networks. Proceedings of the National Academy of Sciences, 107(12), 5334–5338.
- Van der Kolk, B. (2014). The Body Keeps the Score: Brain, Mind, and Body in the Healing of Trauma. New York: Penguin.

Chapter 5: The Power of Small Changes—Unlocking Growth Through Tiny Shifts

Further Reading

- Clear, J. (2018). Atomic Habits: An Easy & Proven Way to Build Good Habits & Break Bad Ones. Avery.
- Duhigg, C. (2012). The Power of Habit: Why We Do What We Do in Life and Business. Random House.
- Siegel, D. J. (2020). The Developing Mind: How Relationships and the Brain Interact to Shape Who We Are (3rd ed.). Guilford Press.

- Dweck, C. (2006). Mindset: The New Psychology of Success. Random House.
- Syed, M. (2015). Black Box Thinking: Why Most People Never Learn from Their Mistakes—But Some Do. Penguin.

Chapter 6: The Power of Precision—Davion's Journey

Further Reading

- Kimbro, D. K. (1997). What Makes the Great Great: Strategies for Extraordinary Achievement. Doubleday.
- Clear, J. (2018). Atomic Habits: An Easy & Proven Way to Build Good Habits & Break Bad Ones. Avery.
- Duhigg, C. (2012). The Power of Habit: Why We Do What We Do in Life and Business. Random House.
- Duckworth, A. (2016). Grit: The Power of Passion and Perseverance. Scribner.
- Coyle, D. (2009). The Talent Code: Greatness Isn't Born. It's Grown. Here's How. Bantam.
- Ericsson, K. A., Krampe, R. T., & Tesch-Römer, C. (1993). The role of deliberate practice in the acquisition of expert performance. Psychological Review, 100(3), 363–406.

Chapter 7: The Subtle Shift—How Tiny Details Sparked My Revival

Further Reading

- Bancroft, L. (2002). Why Does He Do That? Inside the Minds of Angry and Controlling Men. Berkley Books
- Stern, R. (2018). The Gaslight Effect: How to Spot and Survive the Hidden Manipulation Others Use to Control Your Life. Harmony.

- Engel, B. (2002). The Emotionally Abusive Relationship: How to Stop Being Abused and How to Stop Abusing. Wiley.
- National Domestic Violence Hotline. (n.d.). What is Gaslighting?
- Psychology Today. (n.d.). Emotional Abuse

Chapter 8: Business Hinges—The Lines That Hold the Dream

Further Reading

- Gawande, A. (2009). The Checklist Manifesto: How to Get Things Right. Metropolitan Books.
- Clear, J. (2018). Atomic Habits: An Easy & Proven Way to Build Good Habits & Break Bad Ones. Avery.
- Harvard Business Review. (2011). The Power of Small Wins.
- Harvard Business Review. (2002). The Discipline of Paying Attention.
- Indeed.com. (n.d.). Attention to Detail: Definition and Examples.

Chapter 9: The Invisible Architects—Behind the Leaders

Further Reading

- Jones, C. B., & Boyd, S. (2011). Behind the Dream: The Making of the Speech that Transformed a Nation. Palgrave Macmillan.
- Shetterly, M. L. (2016). Hidden Figures: The American Dream and the Untold Story of the Black Women Mathematicians Who Helped Win the Space Race. William Morrow.
- Jarrett, V. (2019). Finding My Voice: My Journey to the West Wing and the Path Forward. Viking.
- Knowles, T. (2025). Matriarch: A Memoir. One World.

- Warner, H., & Hergenrother, A. (2019). The Founder & The Force Multiplier: How Entrepreneurs and Executive Assistants Achieve More Together. Lioncrest Publishing.
- Hochschild, A. R. (2012). The Managed Heart: Commercialization of Human Feeling (Updated ed.). University of California Press.

Chapter 10: Vital Signs—The Habits That Heal

Further Reading

- Ornish, D., & Ornish, A. (2020). Undo It!: How Simple Lifestyle Changes Can Reverse Most Chronic Diseases. Ballantine Books.
- Hyman, M. (2020). Food Fix: How to Save Our Health, Our Economy, Our Communities, and Our Planet – One Bite at a Time. Little, Brown Spark.
- Walker, M. (2017). Why We Sleep: Unlocking the Power of Sleep and Dreams. Scribner.
- Ratey, J. J. (2008). Spark: The Revolutionary New Science of Exercise and the Brain. Little, Brown.

Chapter 11: Becoming Tomorrow—Parenting with the End in Mind Children

Further Reading

- Siegel, D. J., & Bryson, T. P. (2011). The Whole-Brain Child: 12 Revolutionary Strategies to Nurture Your Child's Developing Mind. Delacorte Press.
- Levine, M. (2006). The Price of Privilege: How Parental Pressure and Material Advantage Are Creating a Generation of Disconnected and Unhappy Kids. Harper.

- Coates, T. (2015). Between the World and Me. Spiegel & Grau.
- Kendi, I. X. (2020). Antiracist Baby. Kokila.
- Tatum, B. D. (2017). Why Are All the Black Kids Sitting Together in the Cafeteria? And Other Conversations About Race. Basic Books.
- Goleman, D. (1995). Emotional Intelligence: Why It Can Matter More Than IQ. Bantam Books.
- Steinberg, L. (2014). Age of Opportunity: Lessons from the New Science of Adolescence. Eamon Dolan/Houghton Mifflin Harcourt.
- American Psychological Association. (2023). Parenting Resources and Racial Socialization.

Chapter 12: Composing Clarity—The Discipline of Creativity

Further Reading

- Newport, C. (2016). Deep Work: Rules for Focused Success in a Distracted World. Grand Central Publishing.
- Pressfield, S. (2002). The War of Art: Break Through the Blocks and Win Your Inner Creative Battles. Black Irish Entertainment.
- Csikszentmihalyi, M. (1990). Flow: The Psychology of Optimal Experience. Harper & Row.
- Mamet, D. (1998). True and False: Heresy and Common Sense for the Actor. Vintage.
- Bogart, A. (2001). A Director Prepares: Seven Essays on Art and Theatre. Routledge.

Chapter 13: One Letter at a Time: The Map to Human Connection

Further Reading

- Marston, W. M. (1928). *Emotions of Normal People*. Harcourt, Brace & Co.
- Rohm, R. A. (2005). *Positive Personality Profiles: D-I-S-C-over Personality Insights to Understand Yourself and Others*. Personality Insights, Inc.
- DISC Profile Overview. (n.d.). Retrieved from https://www.discprofile.com/what-is-disc

Chapter 14: The Whisper, Not the Wind

Further Reading

- Blackaby, H. and Blackaby, R (2002). Hearing God's Voice. B&H Publishing.
  — A fresh exploration of how to recognize and respond to God's voice in the modern world.
- Warren, T. H. (2021). Prayer in the Night: For Those Who Work or Watch or Weep. InterVarsity Press.
  — A moving reflection on how prayer sustains us in seasons of grief, doubt, and darkness.
- Kong, C. (2020). How to Hear the Voice of God. Independently published.
  — A practical and personal guide to cultivating spiritual listening and discernment.
- Virkler, M. and Virkler P. (2013). 4 Keys to Hearing God's Voice. Communion With God Ministries.
  — A simple framework to help readers hear God more clearly through stillness, journaling, and inner witness.

- Myers, F. (2023). When God Speaks: Listening to the Voice of God. WestBow Press.
  — Personal stories and biblical insights that illustrate how God uses whispers and impressions to guide us.

- Hagin, K. W. (2014, Rev. Ed.). Listen to Your Heart: Hearing God in a Noisy World. Faith Library Publications.

Chapter 15: The Mustard Seed Effect—How Small Observations Advance Science

Further Reading

- Ried, K. (2020). Garlic lowers blood pressure in hypertensive individuals, regulates serum cholesterol, and stimulates immunity: An updated meta-analysis and review. *The Journal of Nutrition*, 150(7), 1320S–1328S.

- Banerjee, S. K., & Maulik, S. K. (2002). Effect of garlic on cardiovascular disorders: A review. *Nutrition Journal*, 18(6), 709–721.

- Duke, J. A. (2000). *The Green Pharmacy*. Rodale Press.

- Yeh, G. Y., et al. (2006). "Complementary and Alternative Medicine Use Among Adults in the United States." *Alternative Therapies in Health and Medicine*, 12(1), 44–49.]

- Fejes, R., et al. (2024). Exploring the health benefits of raw white garlic consumption in humans: A mini review. Frontiers in Nutrition, 11, 1459627.

Chapter 16: The Algorithm and Me: Javier's Aha Moment

Further Reading

- Allen, J. (2017). As a Man Thinketh: 21st Century Edition. Edited by Sam Torode. Independently Published.

- Zuboff, S. (2020). The Age of Surveillance Capitalism: The Fight for a Human Future at the New Frontier of Power. PublicAffairs.
- Tufekci, Z. (2017). Twitter and Tear Gas: The Power and Fragility of Networked Protest. Yale University Press.
- Noble, S. U. (2018). Algorithms of Oppression: How Search Engines Reinforce Racism. NYU Press.
- Orlowski, J. (Director). (2020). The Social Dilemma [Film]. Netflix.
- Marwick, A., & Lewis, R. (2017). Media Manipulation and Disinformation Online. Data & Society Research Institute.
- Center for Humane Technology. (2021). Ledger of Harms. [Online resource].

Chapter 17: Modern Echoes — How Small Digital Acts Fuel Movements Today

Further Reading

- Frazier, D. (2021). Pulitzer Special Citation Announcement. Pulitzer.org. https://www.pulitzer.org
- Wells, I. B. (2014). The Light of Truth: Writings of an Anti-Lynching Crusader. Penguin Classics.
- Gbowee, L. (2011). Mighty Be Our Powers: How Sisterhood, Prayer, and Sex Changed a Nation at War. Beast Books.
- Kendi, I. X. (2019). How to Be an Antiracist. One World Essentials.
- Thunberg, G. (2019). No One Is Too Small to Make a Difference. Penguin UK.
- González, E. (2018). March for Our Lives Speech. Available via CSPAN archives: https://www.c-span.org/video/?442681-1

- Stevenson, B. (2015). Just Mercy: A Story of Justice and Redemption. One World.

Chapter 18: The Quiet Redline—Housing Discrimination

Further Reading

- Rothstein, R. (2018). The Color of Law: A Forgotten History of How Our Government Segregated America. Liveright.
- Coates, T. (2014). The Case for Reparations. The Atlantic. [Available online]
- Perry, A., Rothwell, J., and Harshbarger, D., Brookings Institution. (2018). The Devaluation of Assets in Black Neighborhoods: The Case of Residential Property.
- Desmond, M. (2023). Poverty, by America. Crown Publishing.
- Mapping Inequality Project. (University of Richmond). [https://dsl.richmond.edu/panorama/redlining/]
- Aaronson, D., Mazumder B., and Hartley D., Federal Reserve Bank of Chicago. (2021). New Data on Thousands of U.S. Neighborhoods Shows Direct Impact of Redlining from 1930 to Today. [ChicagoFed.org]

Chapter 19: Redacted Memory—The Quiet War on Truth

Further Reading

- Kendi, Ibram X. Stamped from the Beginning: The Definitive History of Racist Ideas in America. 2017.
- Alexander, Michelle. The New Jim Crow: Mass Incarceration in the Age of Colorblindness. New York: The New Press, 2010.
- Civic Memory Working Group. Past Due: Report and Recommendations of the Los Angeles Civic Memory Working

Group. Los Angeles: Office of Mayor Eric Garcetti, 2021. https://civicmemory.la/report

- PEN America. Banned in the USA: The Growing Movement to Censor Books in Schools. New York: PEN America, 2024.
- Southern Poverty Law Center. Teaching Hard History: A Framework for Teaching American Slavery. Montgomery, AL: SPLC, 2018.

Chapter 20: The Memory We Inherit—How Civic Memory Shapes Democracy

Further Reading

- Blight, David W. Frederick Douglass: Prophet of Freedom. New York: Simon & Schuster, 2018.
- Coates, Ta-Nehisi. Between the World and Me. New York: Spiegel & Grau (formerly an imprint of Penguin Random House), 2015.
- Equal Justice Initiative. Public Symbols of the Confederacy. Montgomery, AL: EJI, 2023. Retrieved from https://eji.org
- Hannah Jones, Nikole. The 1619 Project: A New Origin Story. New York: One World (an imprint of Random House), 2021.Monument Lab. National Monument Audit. Retrieved from https://monumentlab.com
- National Museum of African American History and Culture. Talking About Race. Smithsonian Institution. Retrieved from https://nmaahc.si.edu/learn/talking-about-race
- Savage, Kirk. Monument Wars: Washington, D.C., the National Mall, and the Transformation of the Memorial Landscape. Berkeley: University of California Press, 2011.

- Wilkerson, Isabel. Caste: The Origins of Our Discontents. New York: Random House, 2020.
- Pulitzer Center. Tulsa: The Fire and the Forgotten. PBS Documentary, 2021. Available at https://www.pbs.org
- American Historical Association. "Current Threats to Academic Freedom." Perspectives on History, October 2023. Retrieved from https://www.historians.org/publications-and-directories/perspectives-on-history

Chapter 21: A Lens on Little Things—Stories That Shift the World

Further Reading

- The spiraling debt trapping Pakistan's brick kiln workers. Al Jazeera. Retrieved from https://www.aljazeera.com/features/2019/10/21/the-spiralling-debt-trapping-pakistans-brick-kiln-workers (2019)
- Humans of New York blogger Brandon Stanton writes a letter to Donald Trump. CBS News. Retrieved from https://www.cbsnews.com/news/humans-of-new-york-blogger-brandon-stanton-writes-letter-to-donald-trump/ (2016)
- One refugee's dreams of life in America—with Humans of NY storyteller Brandon Stanton. CNN Press Room. Retrieved from https://cnnpressroom.blogs.cnn.com/2015/12/14/one-refugees-dreams-of-life-in-america-with-humansofny-storyteller-brandon-stanton/ (2015)
- Two years after 'Humans of New York,' Brooklyn principal Nadia Lopez is still inspiring students. Glamour. Retrieved from https://www.glamour.com/story/humans-of-new-york-principal-nadia-lopez (2017)

- How a 'Humans of New York' blog post inspired a principal to change her students' lives. PBS NewsHour. Retrieved from https://www.pbs.org/newshour/education/can-done-everywhere-principal-inspired-1-1-million-fundraiser (2015)
- The Pakistani women brick-makers enslaved by debt. TIME. Retrieved from https://time.com/16225/the-pakistani-women-brick-makers-enslaved-by-debt/ (2014)
- Humans of New York' focuses on refugees – Fareed Zakaria interview. YouTube. Retrieved from https://www.youtube.com/watch?v=OQAongV92fk (2015)

Chapter 22: Legacy—What Will They Remember?

Further Reading

- Biography and legacy (Maya Angelou). Biography.com. Retrieved from https://www.biography.com/writer/maya-angelou (2025)
- Learn about Malala Yousafzai. Malala Fund. Retrieved from https://malala.org/malala (2013)
- Her legacy. Mother Teresa of Calcutta Center. Retrieved from https://www.motherteresa.org (2016)
- His life and legacy. Nelson Mandela Foundation. Retrieved from https://www.nelsonmandela.org/content/page/biography (1999)
- Rosa Parks. History.com. Retrieved from https://www.history.com/topics/black-history/rosa-parks (2020)
- C. S. Lewis, in The Weight of Glory, reflects on the eternal significance of human dignity and the unseen value of everyday faithfulness.
- Desmond and Mpho Tutu's The Book of Forgiving invites us to consider legacy through healing, showing how forgiveness can ripple across generations.

- Simon Sinek's Start with Why challenges readers to live from purpose, arguing that people remember not what we do, but why we do it.
- Malala Yousafzai, in I Am Malala, offers a living legacy—one of courage, conviction, and a voice that changed the world before adulthood.

About the Author

Dr. Danita Johnson Woods is a nationally recognized healthcare executive, author, speaker, and entrepreneur whose life's work bridges purpose and impact. Through her leadership, keynote addresses, writing, and philanthropic efforts, she inspires individuals to dream boldly and embrace the power of personal responsibility as a pathway to success.

As President and Chief Executive Officer of Edgewater Health in Gary, Indiana, Dr. Woods leads one of the region's most dynamic integrated healthcare systems, offering behavioral health, primary care, and child welfare services to residents across Northwest Indiana. With a proven track record in organizational turnaround, she is known for breathing new life into struggling institutions—reviving operations while restoring hope and dignity to the communities they serve. Her overarching mission is to make a measurable difference in community health and well-being.

Dr. Woods is the recipient of numerous honors, including the Distinguished Hoosier Award from the Governor of Indiana and induction into the Northwest Indiana Business & Industry Hall of Fame.

A lifelong learner, she holds bachelor's and master's degrees in Public Administration from Indiana University, a master's degree in Social Service Administration and a Graduate Certificate in Health Administration and Policy from the University of Chicago, and a Ph.D. from Walden University.

Her influence extends beyond the boardroom. Dr. Woods is an active voice in national and local civic life, serving on multiple boards and advisory councils across the country. She is guided by a personal mission:

"To lead, teach, and inspire as many people as possible, for as long as possible, to live their best lives."

Beyond her professional accomplishments, Danita is a woman of many passions. She is an avid runner and fitness enthusiast who has completed six marathons. She is also an award-winning porcelain doll artist and collector with a cherished collection of over 300 dolls. Her love for gardening keeps her grounded, even as her leadership takes her to great heights.

She was married to the late Michael Woods, and together they share three children and several grandchildren.

How to Work with Dr. Danita Johnson Woods

Dr. Danita Johnson Woods is a powerful voice for transformation—combining deep experience, candid storytelling, and actionable strategies to help individuals and organizations unlock their full potential.

Whether you are planning a leadership summit, women's empowerment event, health-focused conference, or a team development workshop, Danita delivers high-impact, interactive experiences that inspire change and spark lasting growth. Her keynotes and sessions blend humor, heart, and hard-earned wisdom on topics such as:

- Purposeful Leadership
- Women and Empowerment
- Building Resilient Teams
- Mental and Physical Well-Being
- Community Transformation through Small Actions

Danita is dedicated to helping people lead, live, and serve with clarity and intention. Her presentations are known for being engaging, insightful, and deeply relevant—with every audience walking away with practical tools and renewed inspiration.

If you're looking for a speaker or workshop leader who will captivate your audience and leave a lasting impression, reach out today to book Dr. Danita Johnson Woods.

Let's Work Together

Email: drdanitaj@gmail.com

Website: www.DrDanitaJohnsonWoods.com